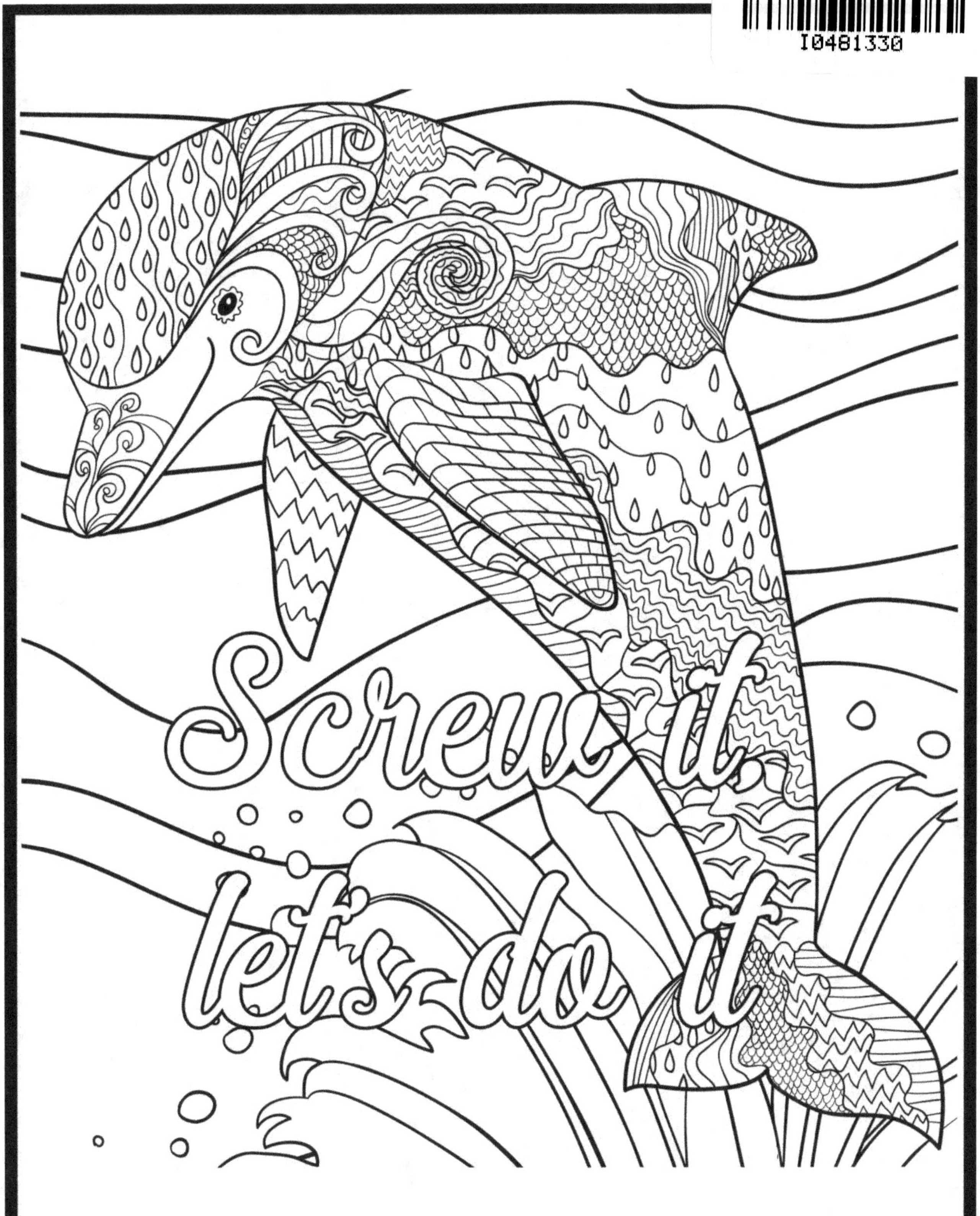

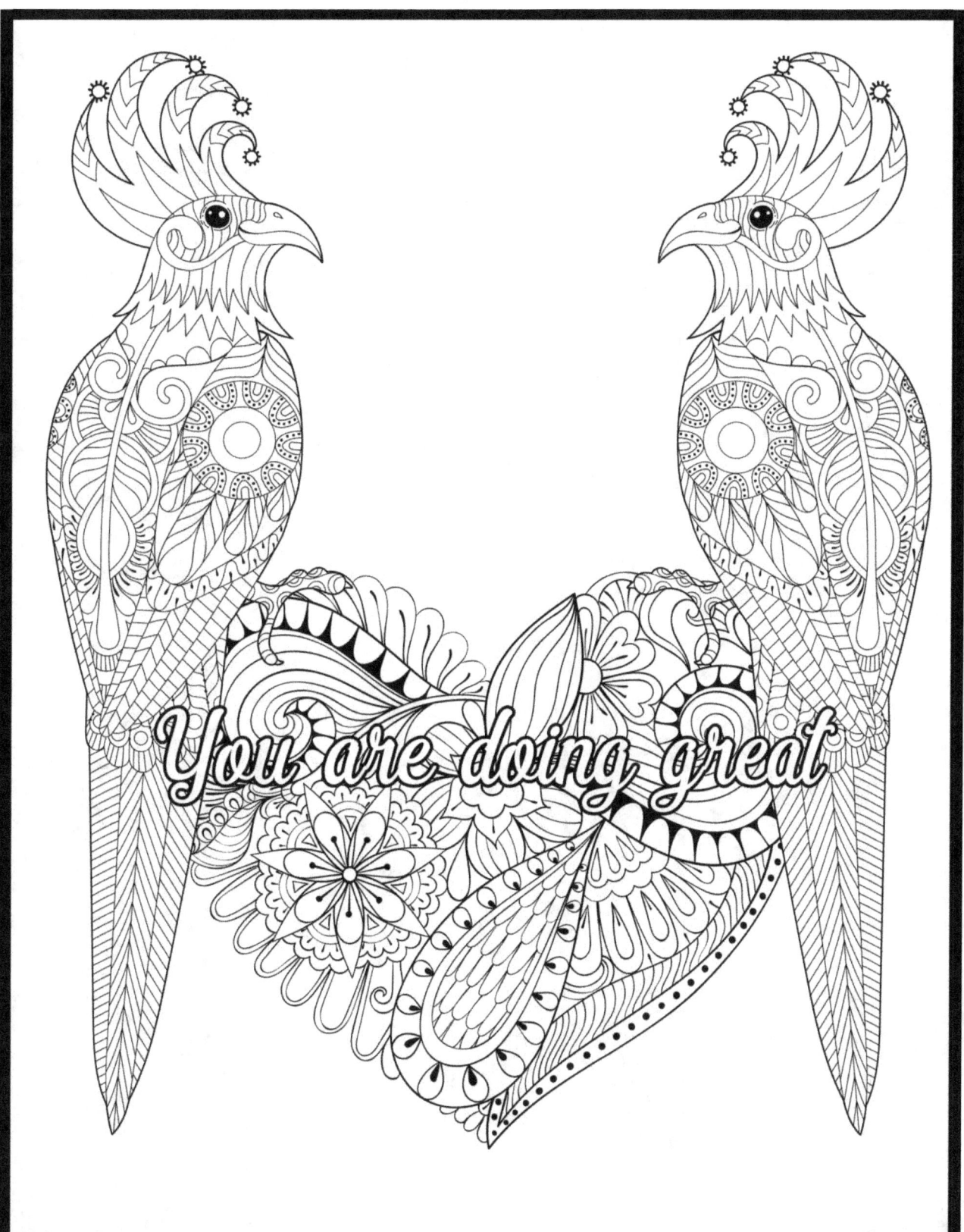

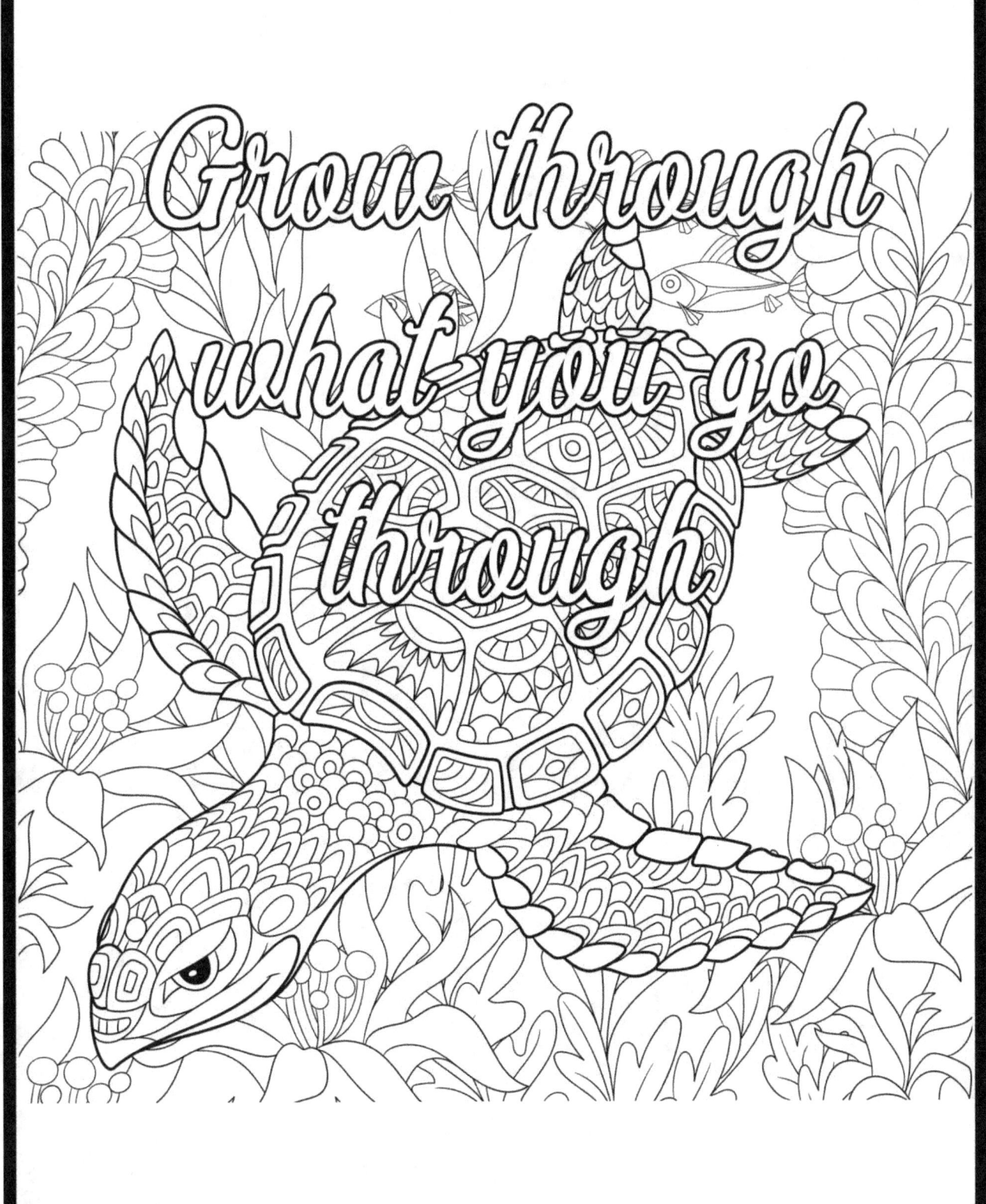

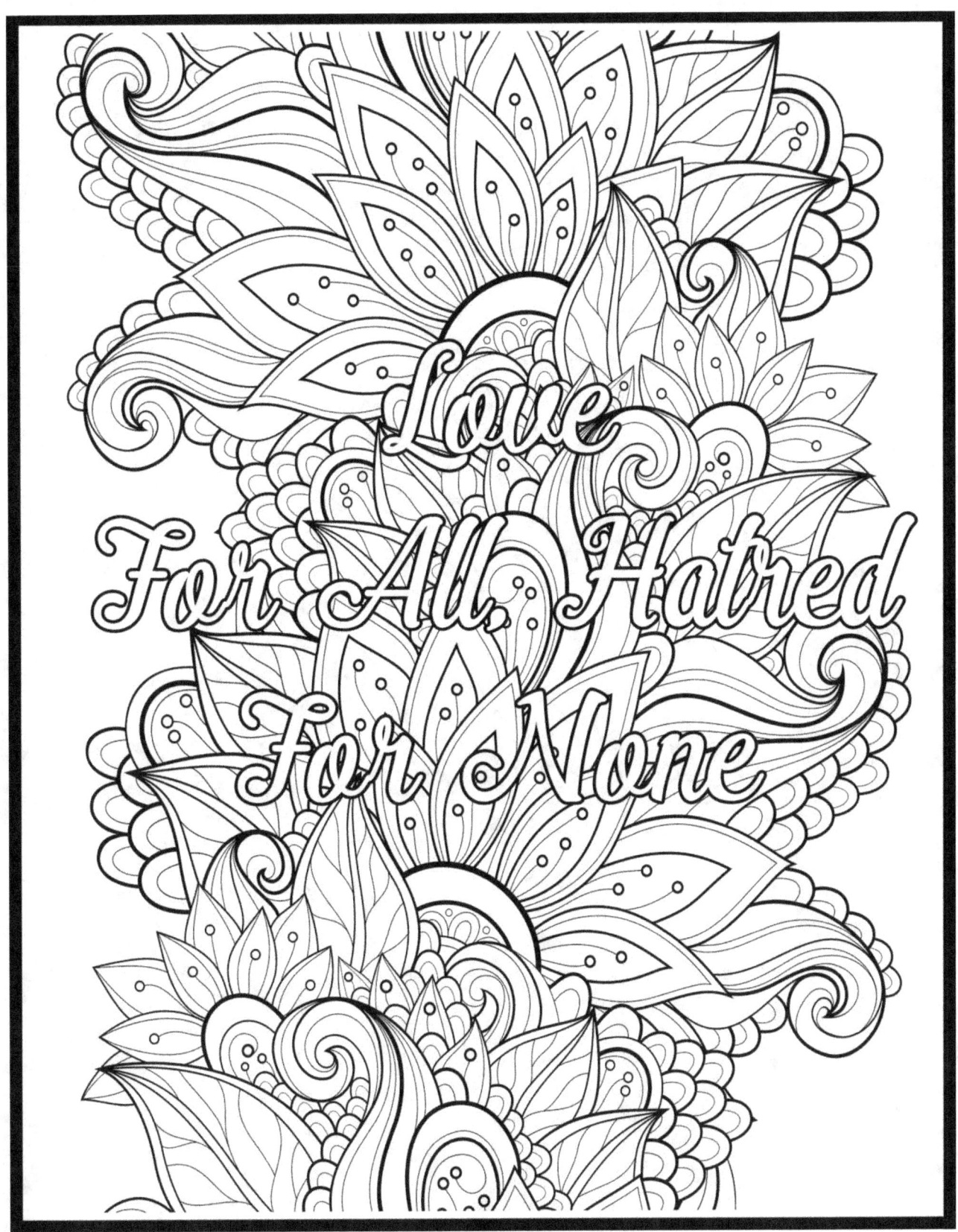

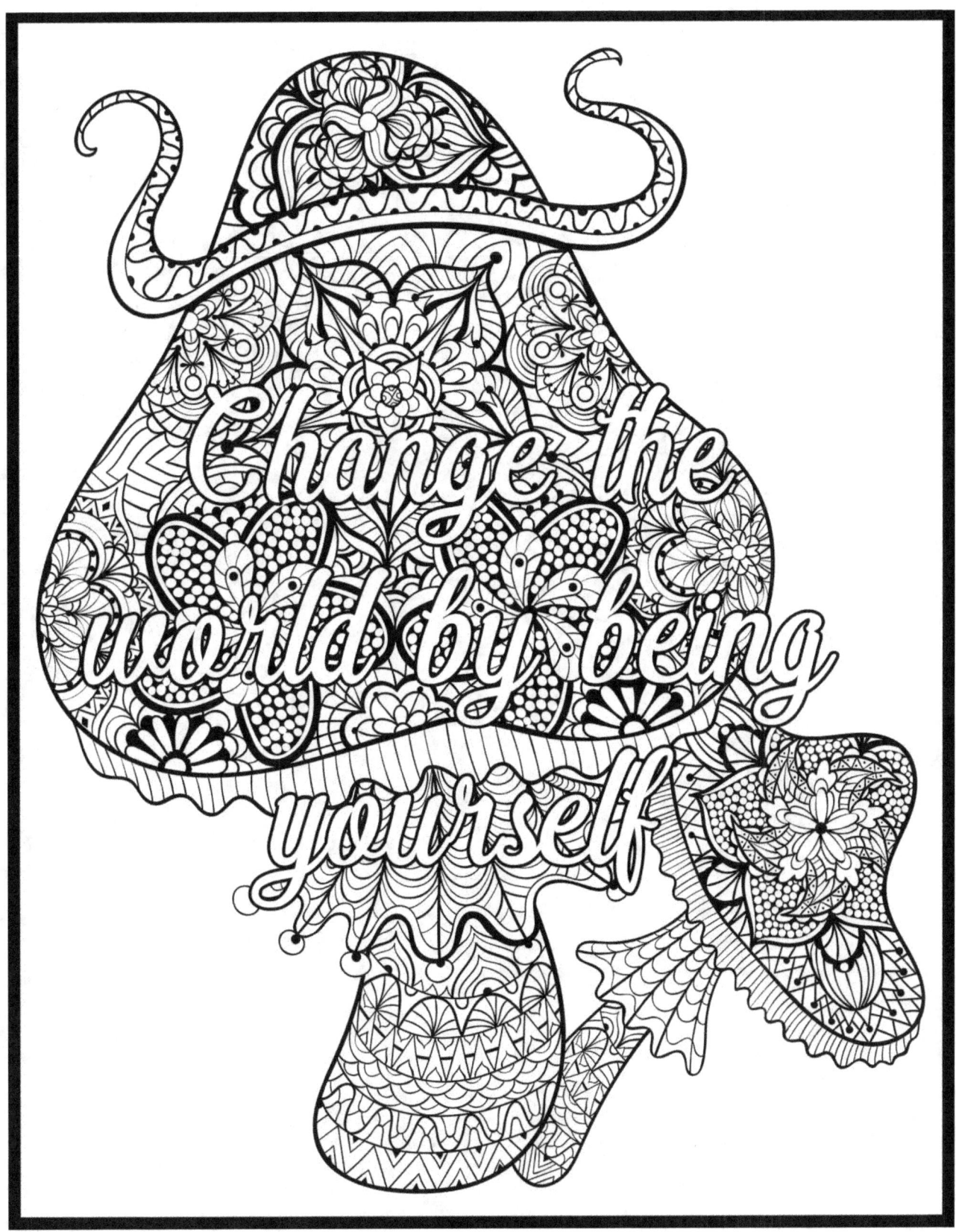

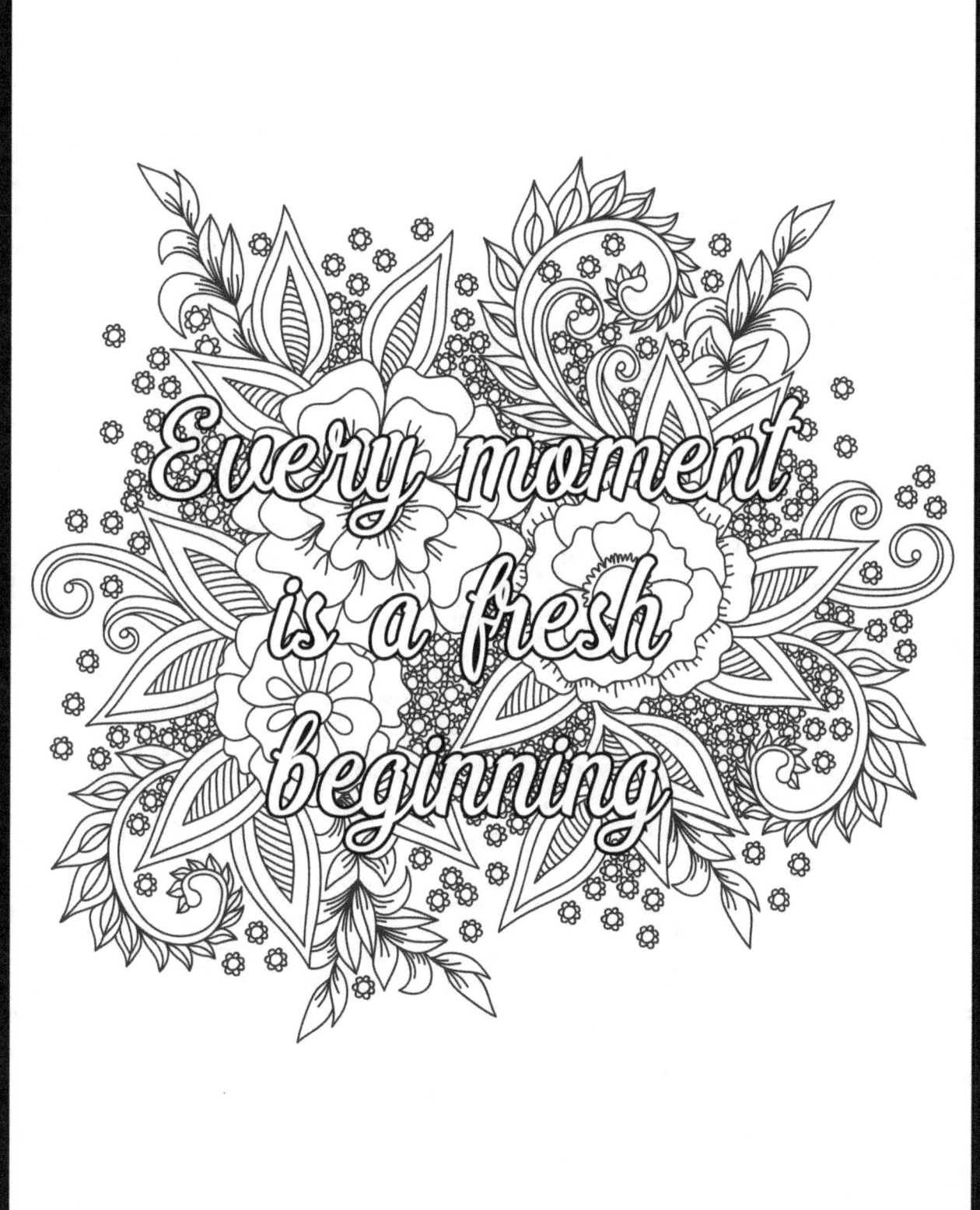

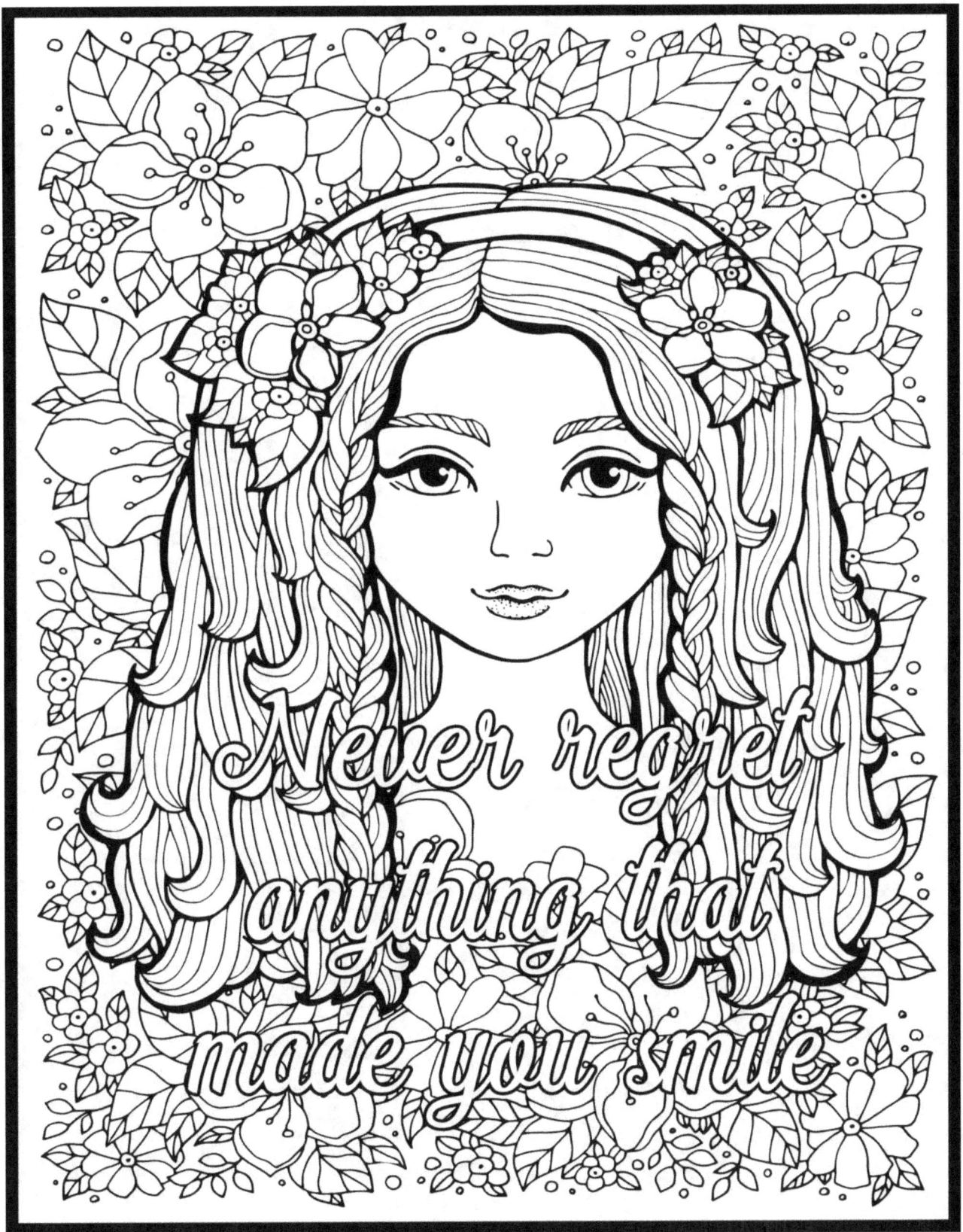

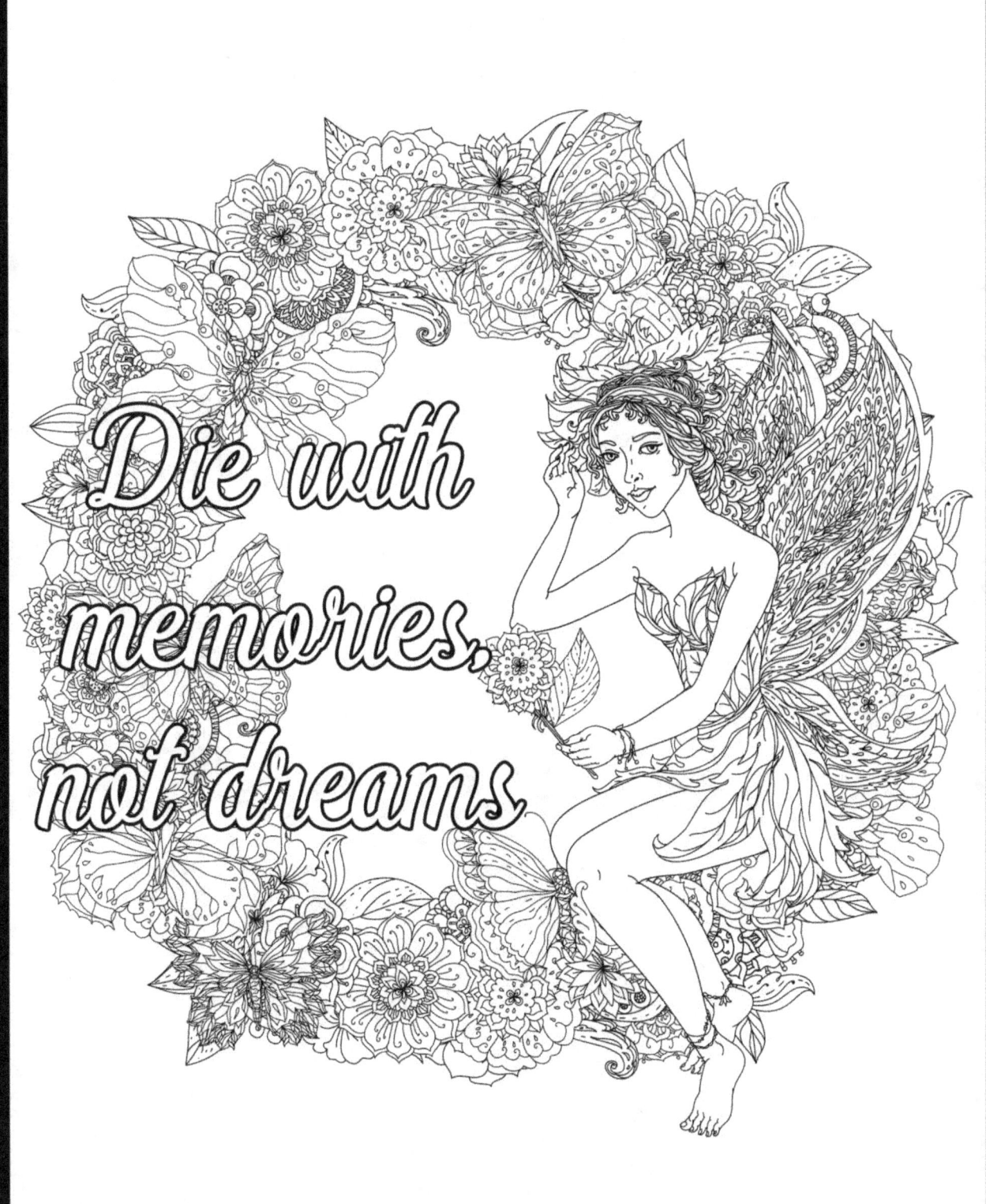

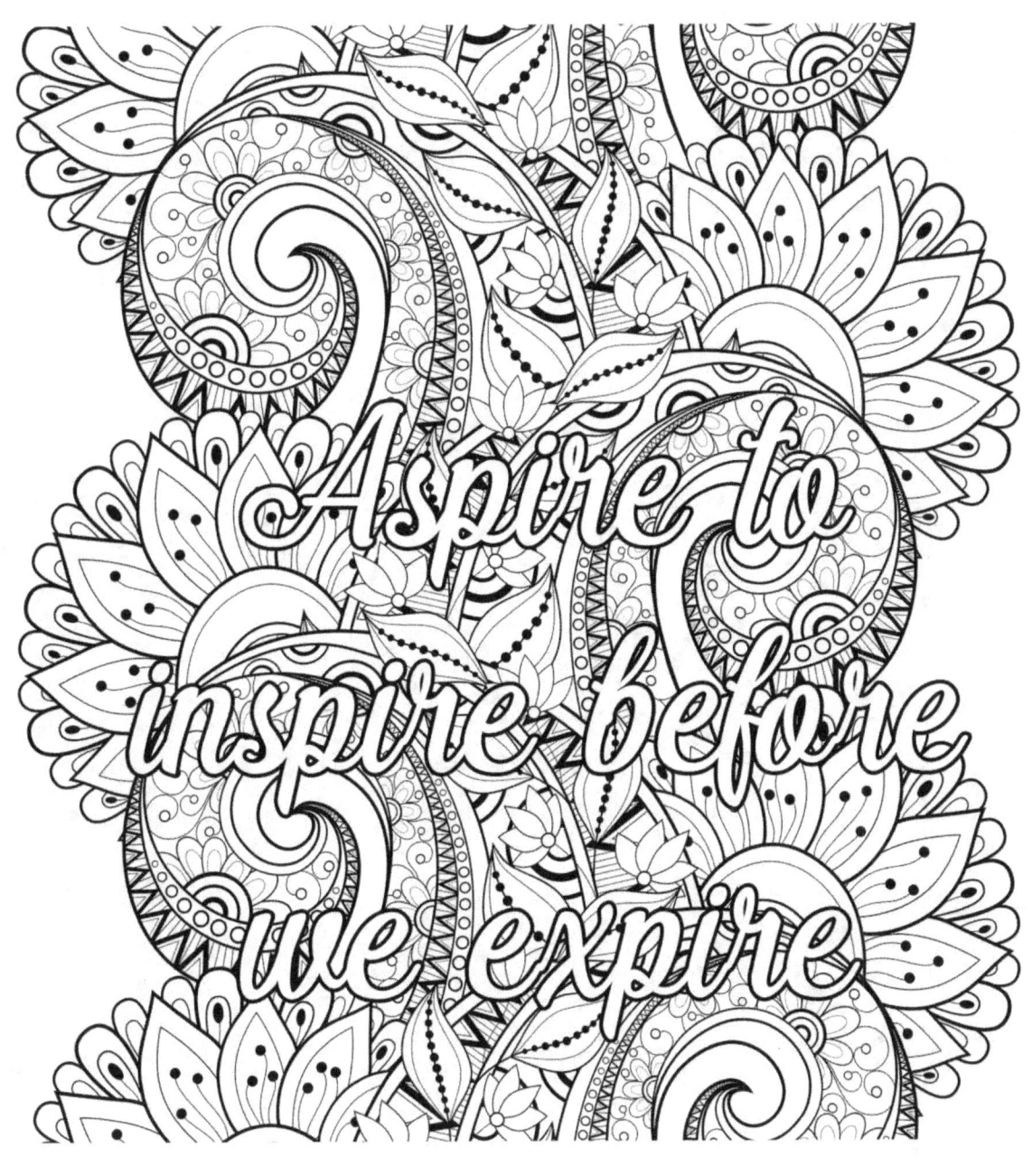

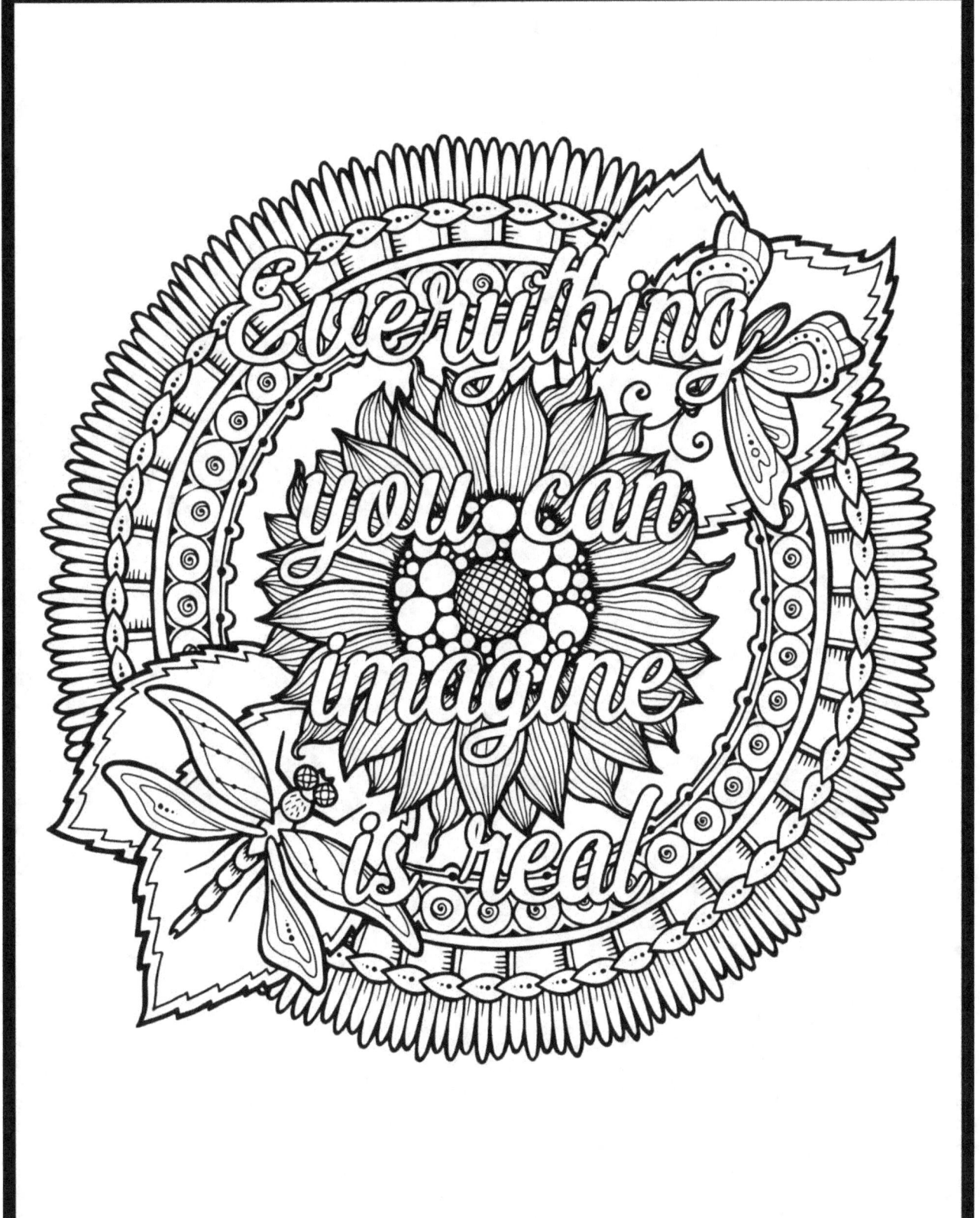

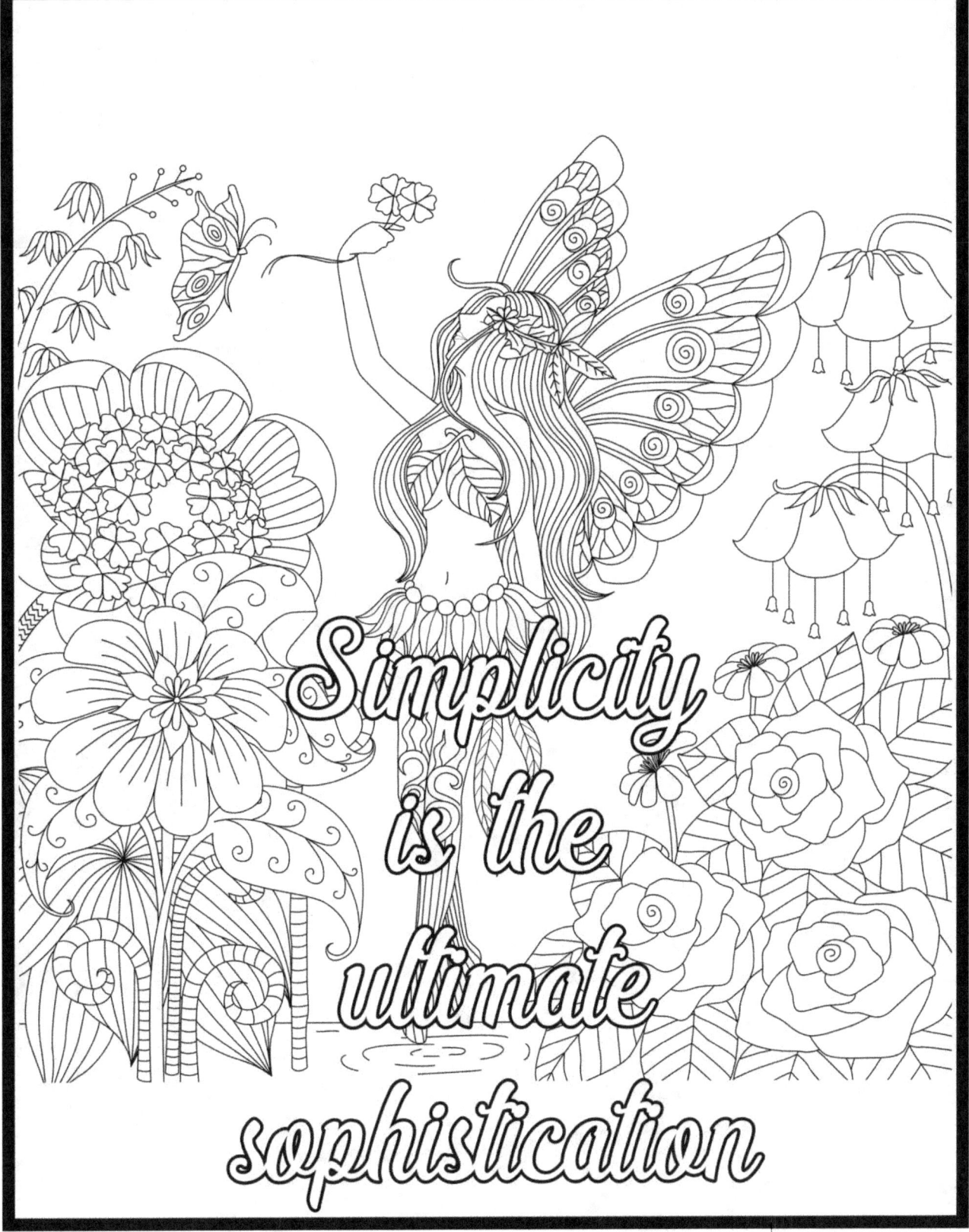

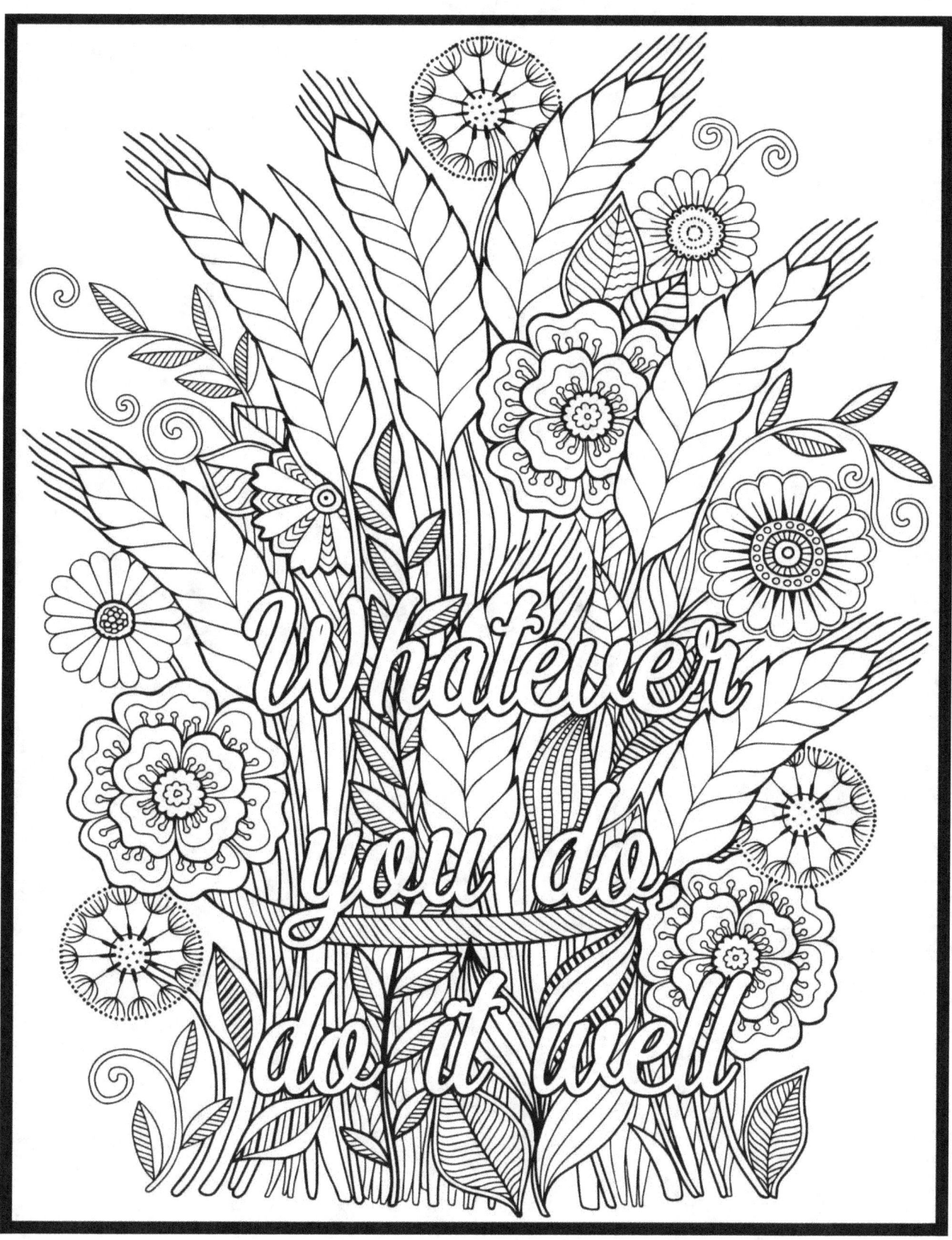

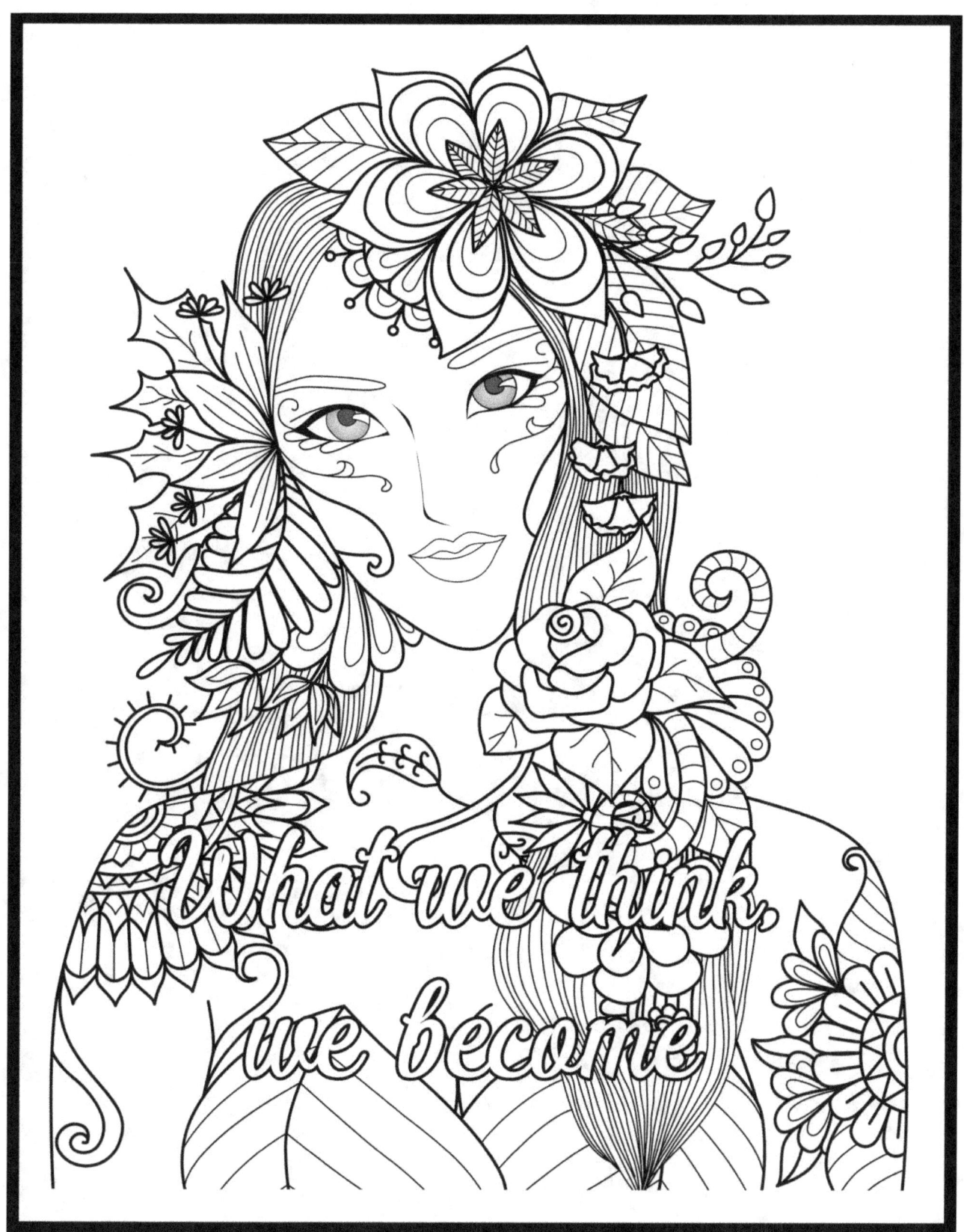

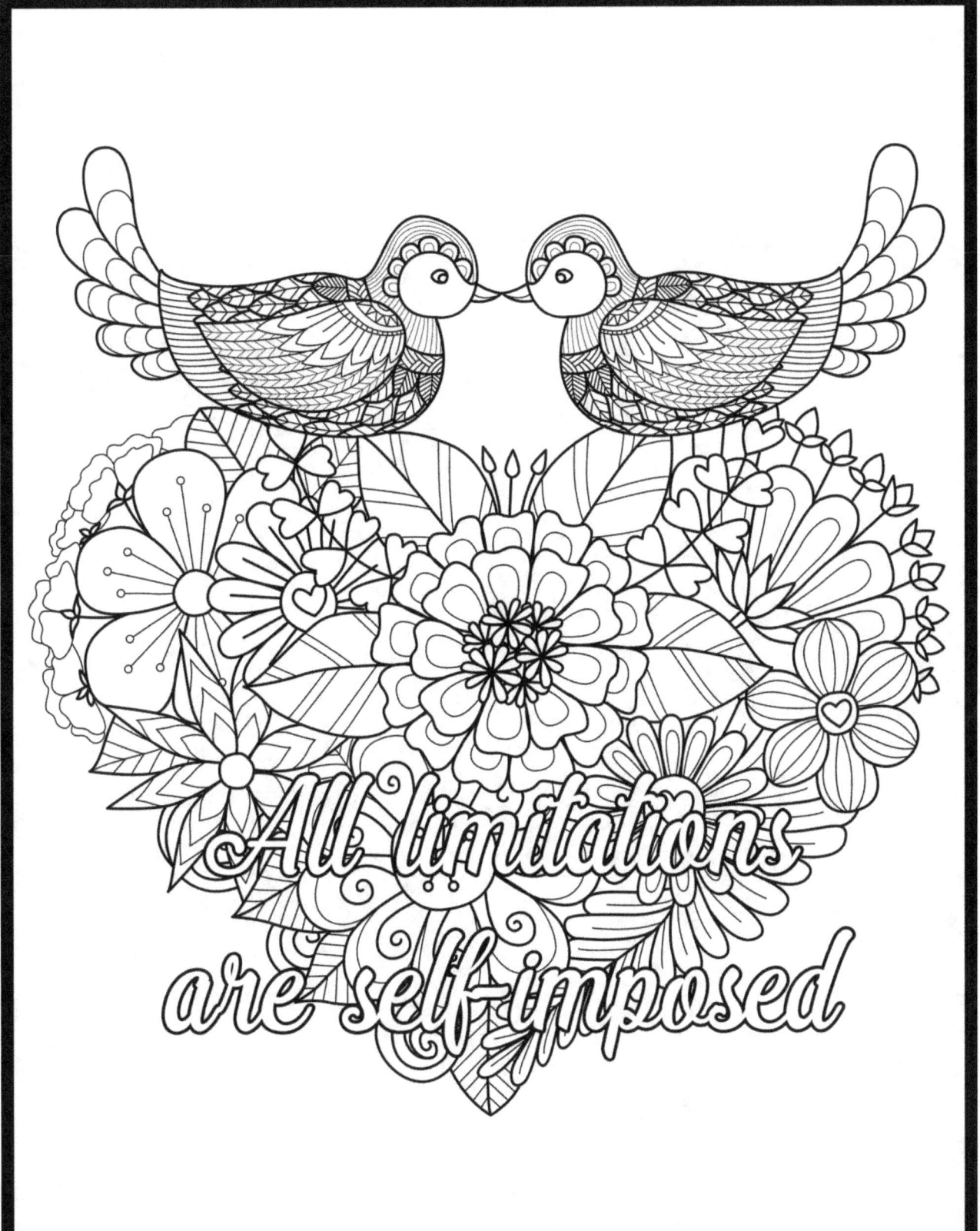

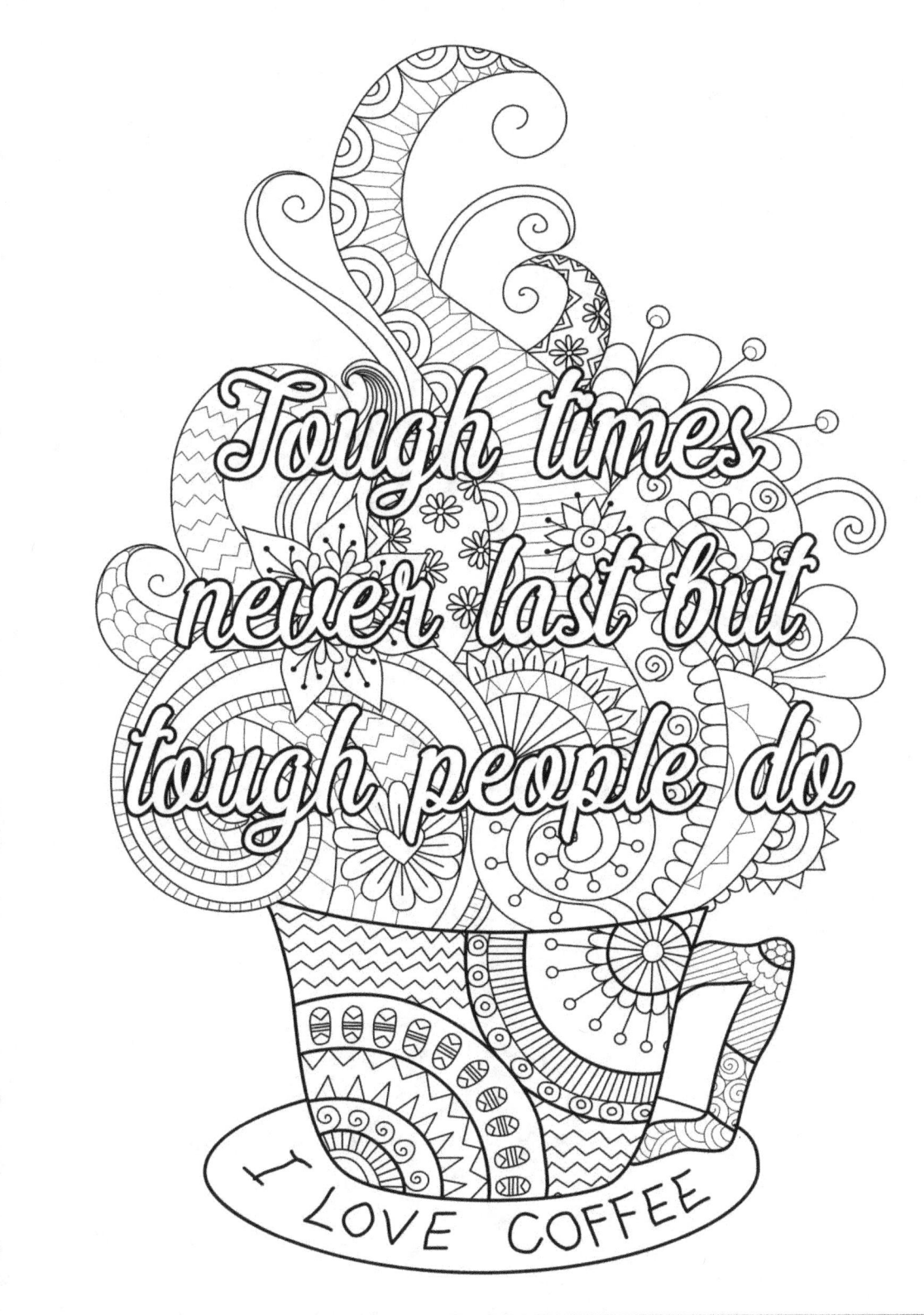

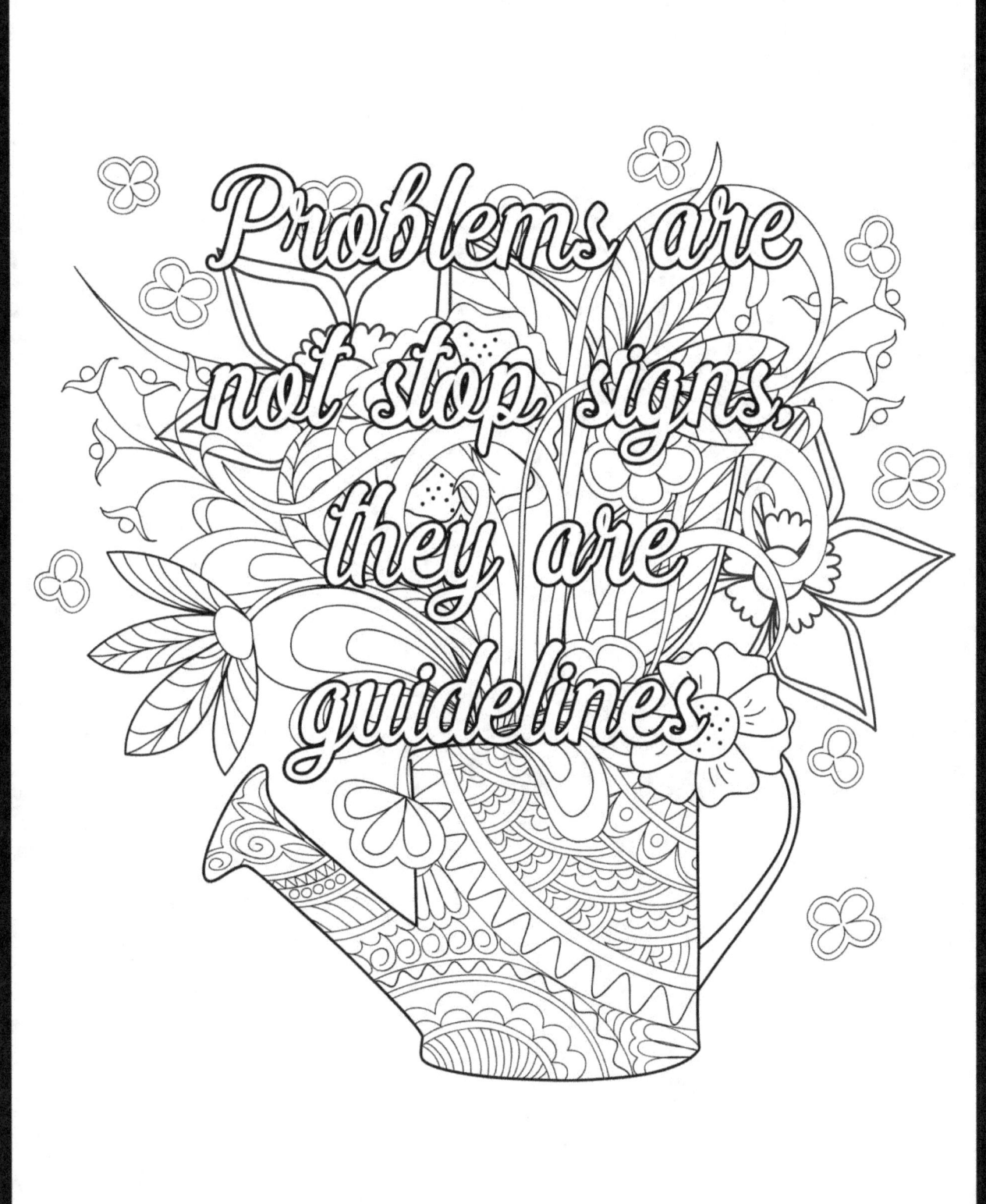

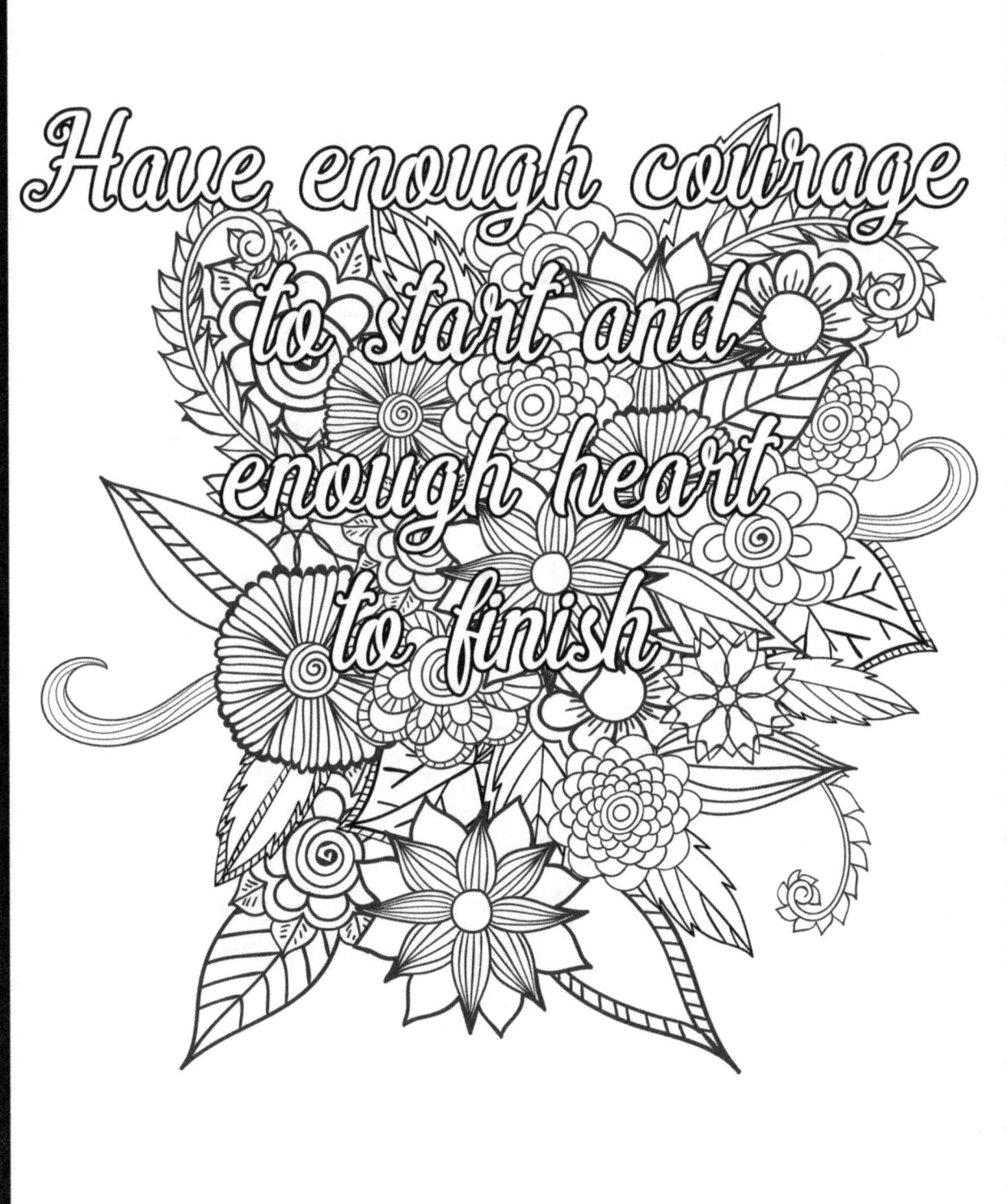

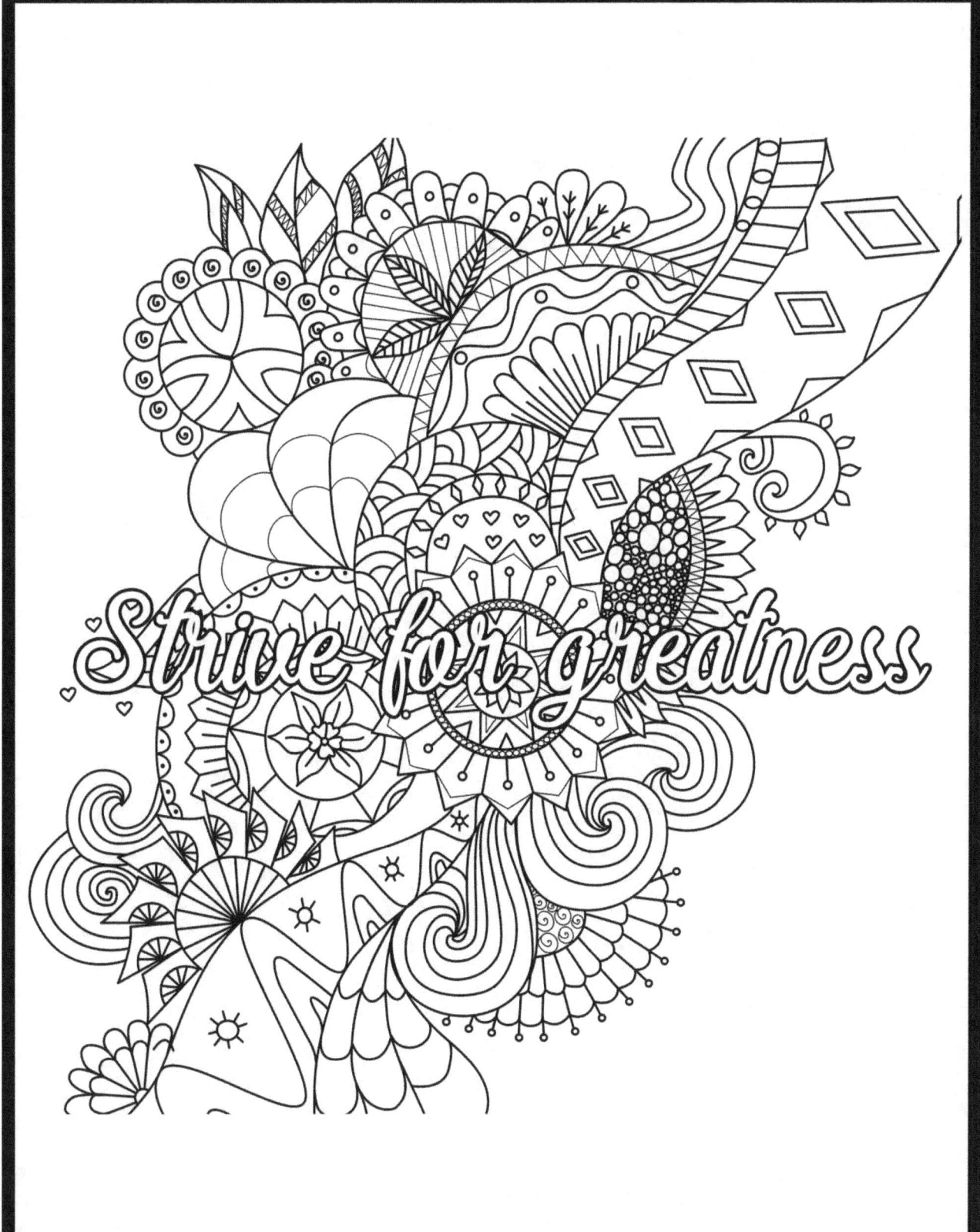

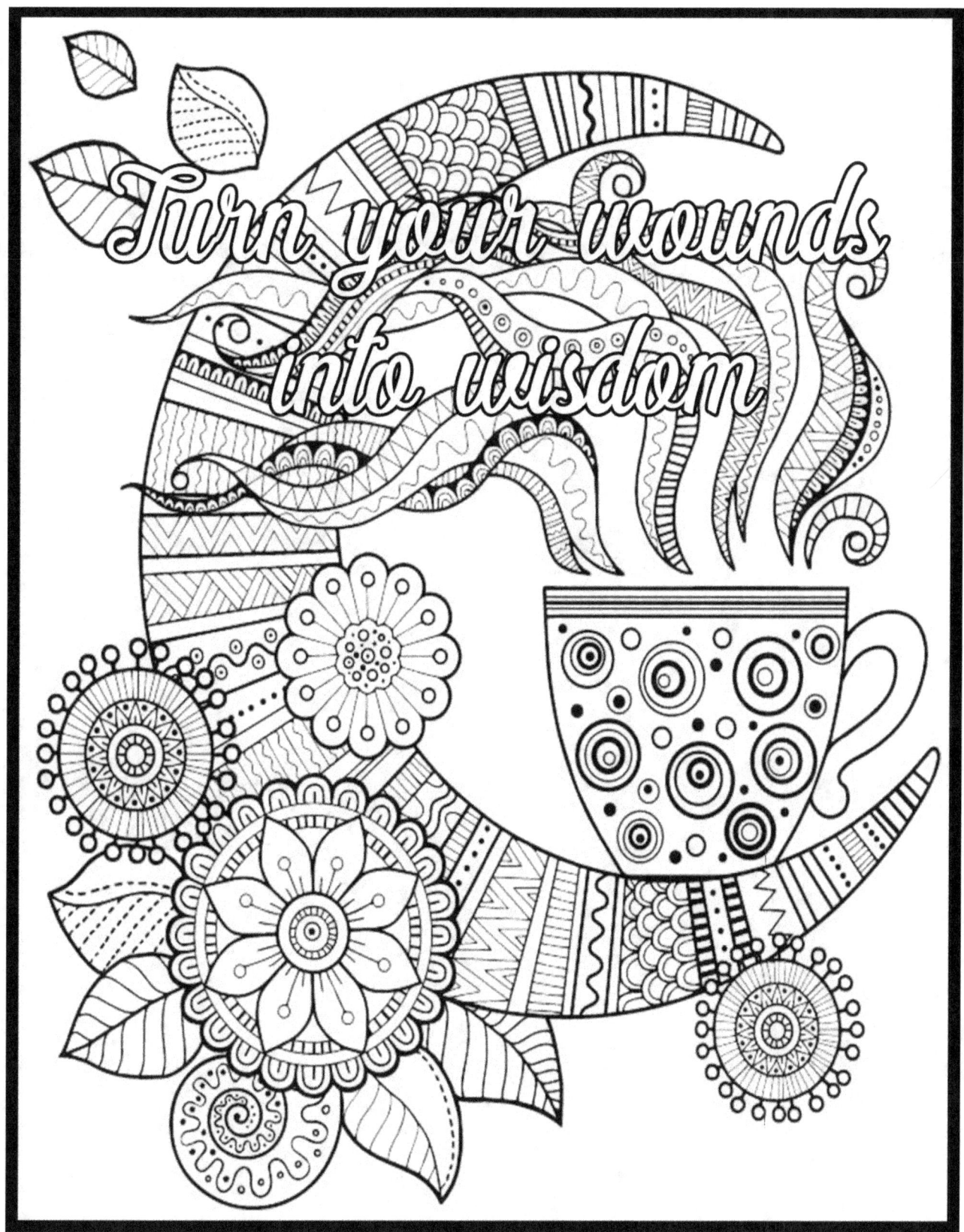

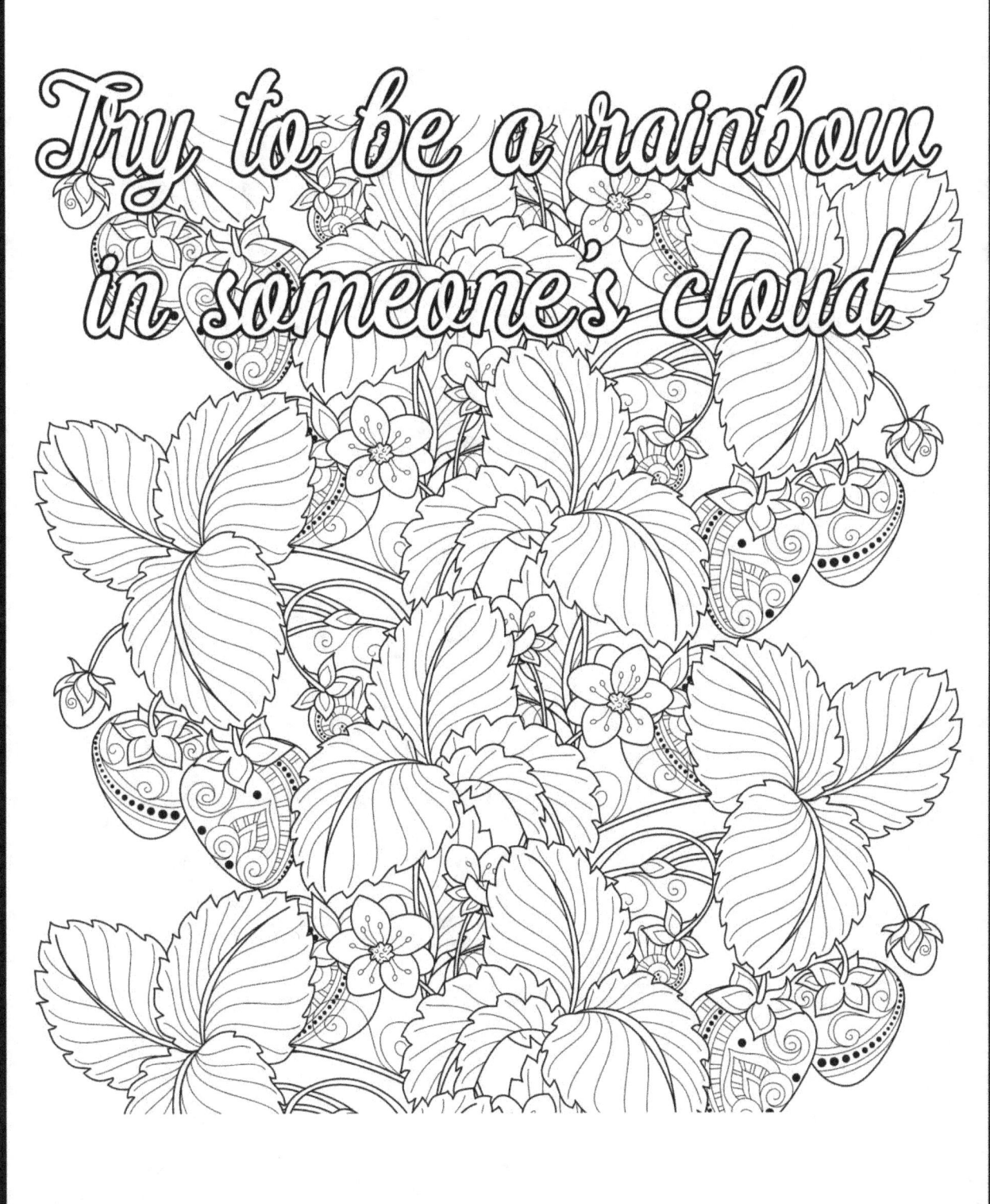

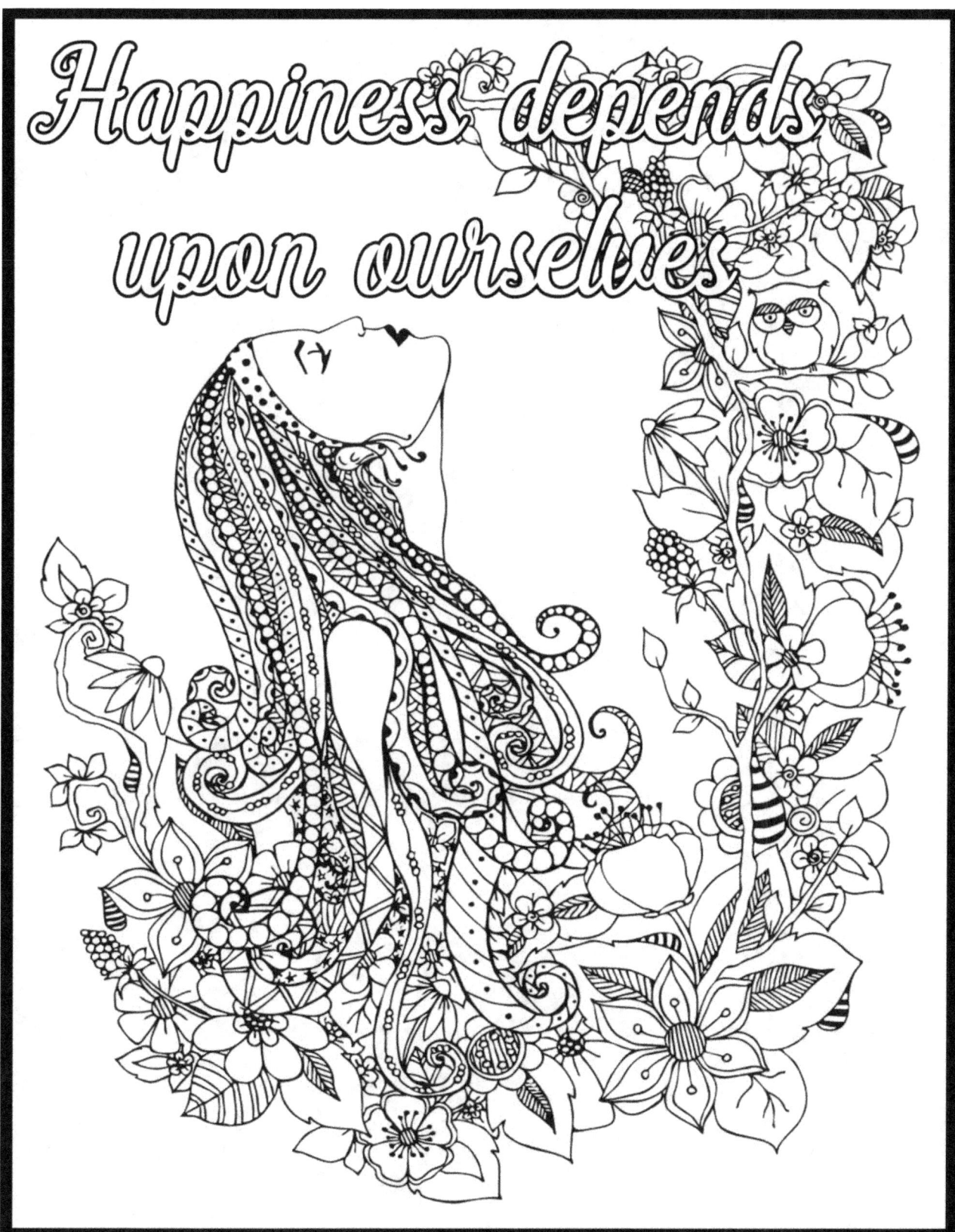

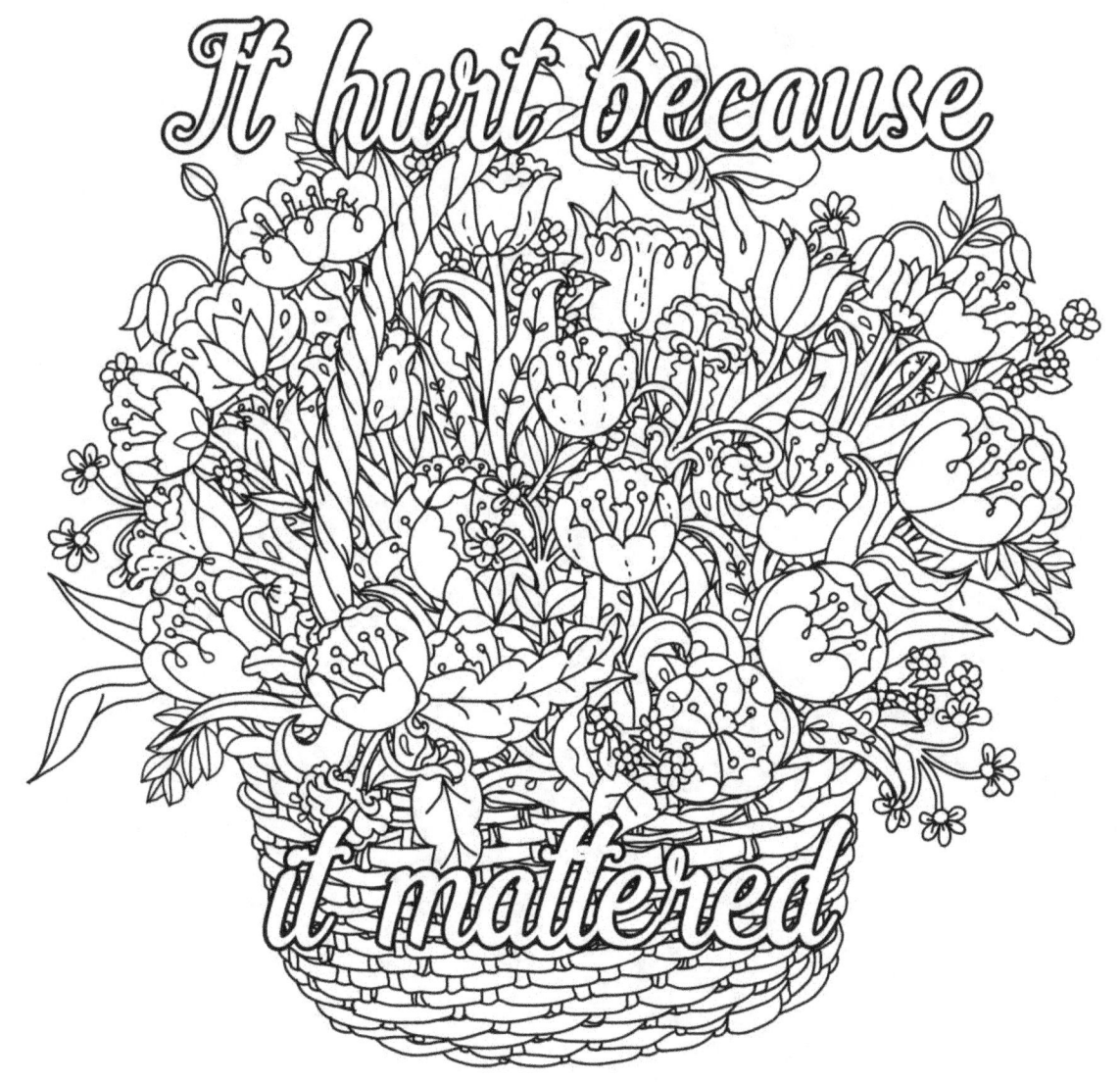

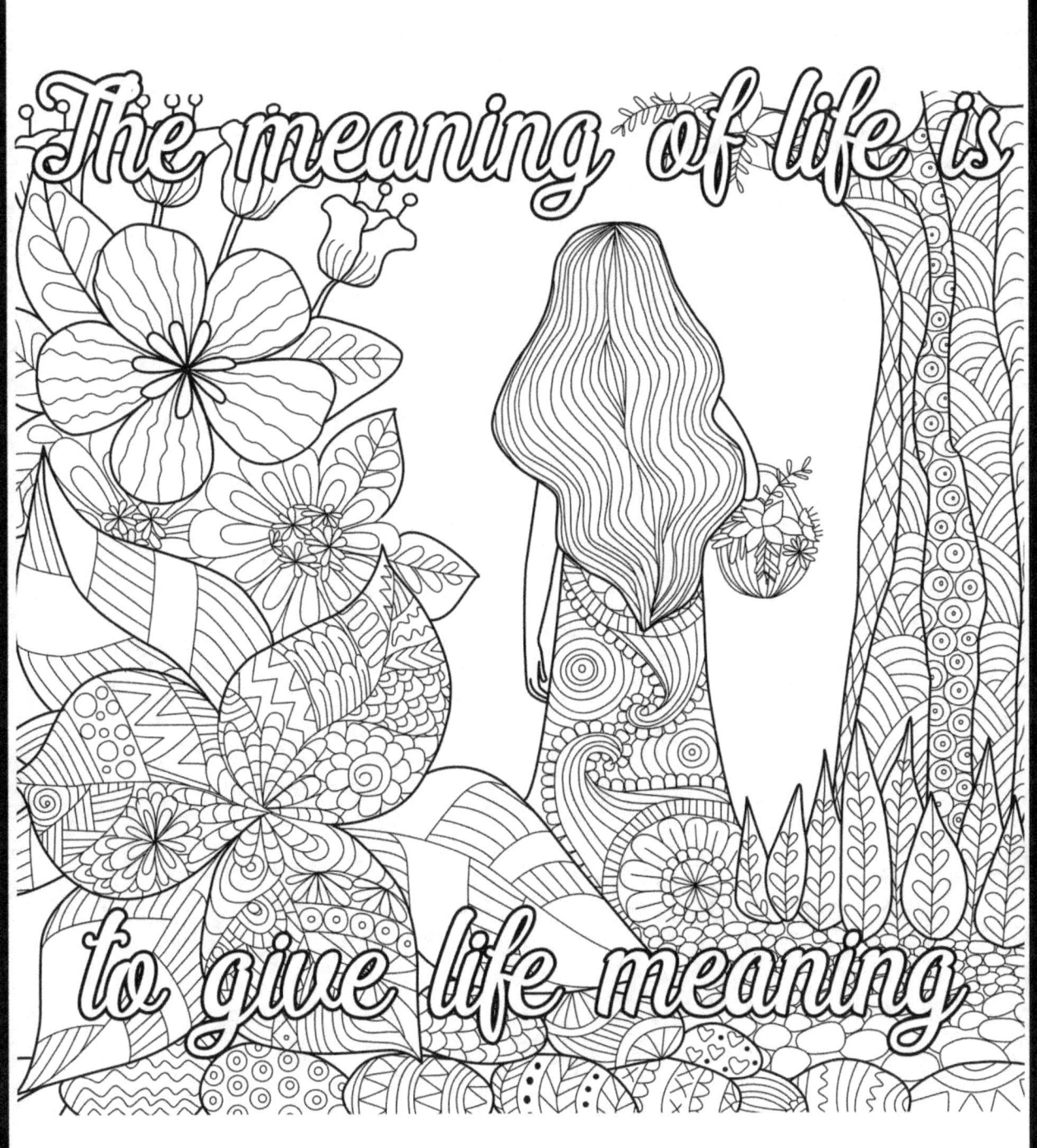

Be yourself,
everyone else
is already taken

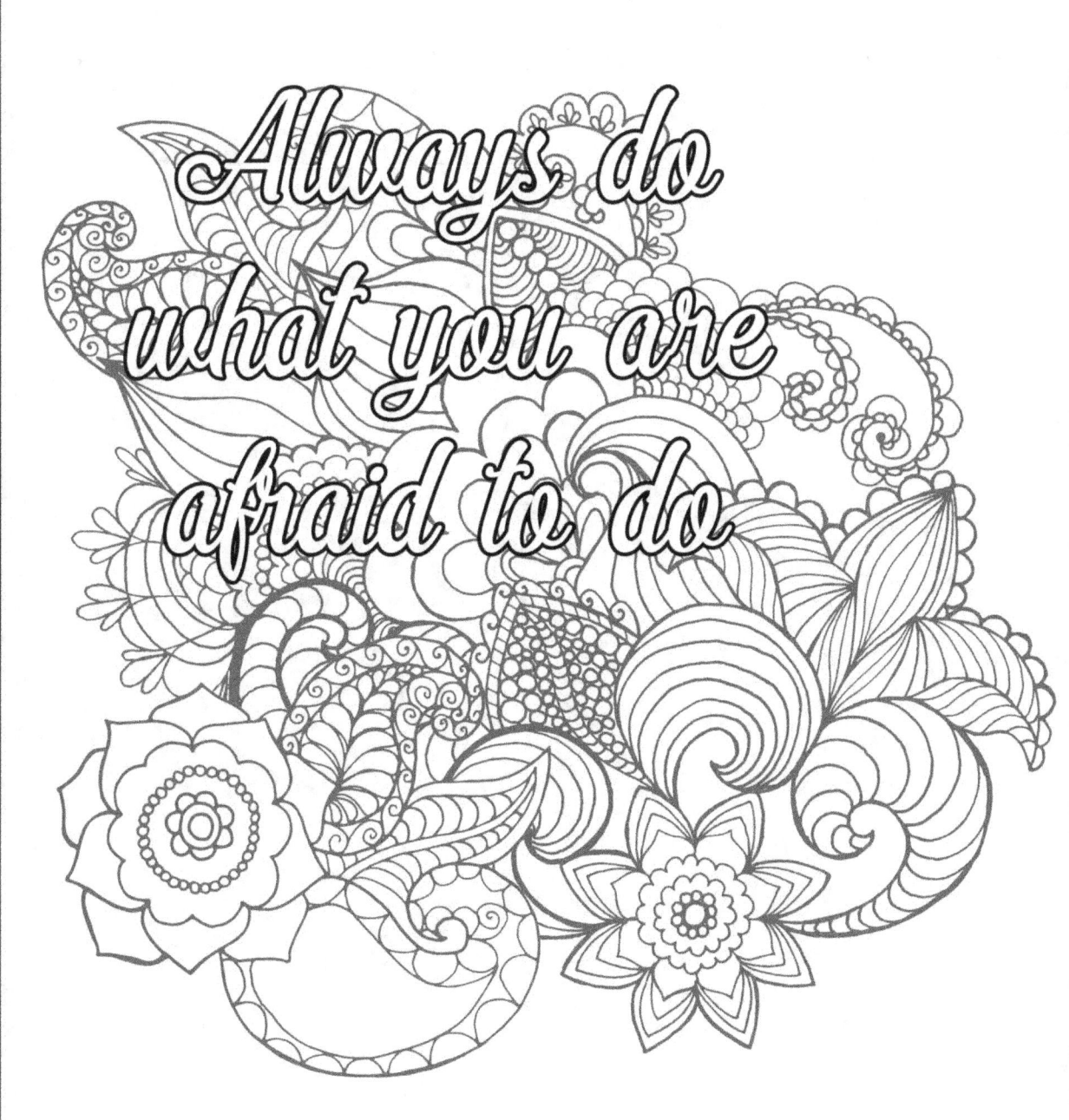

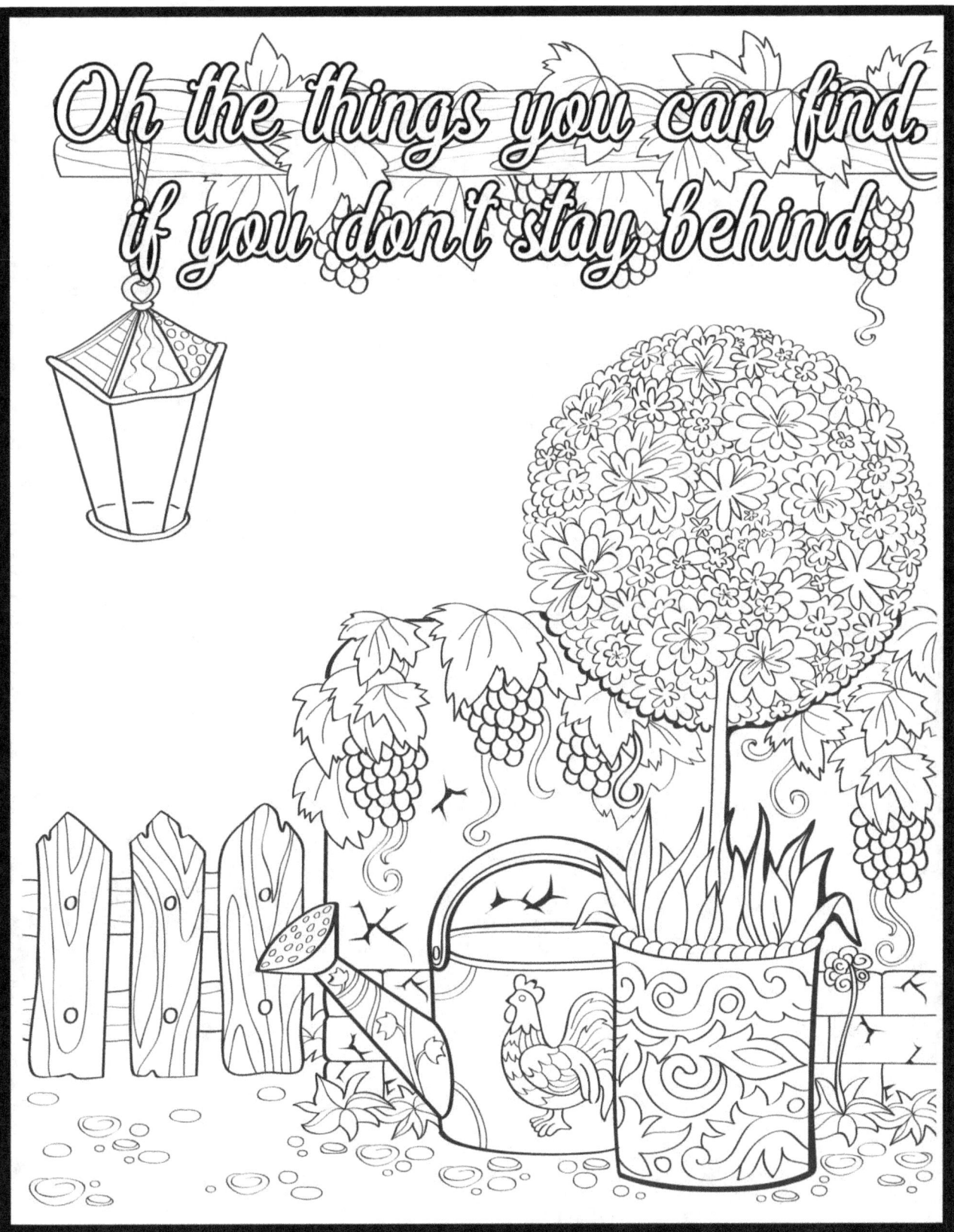

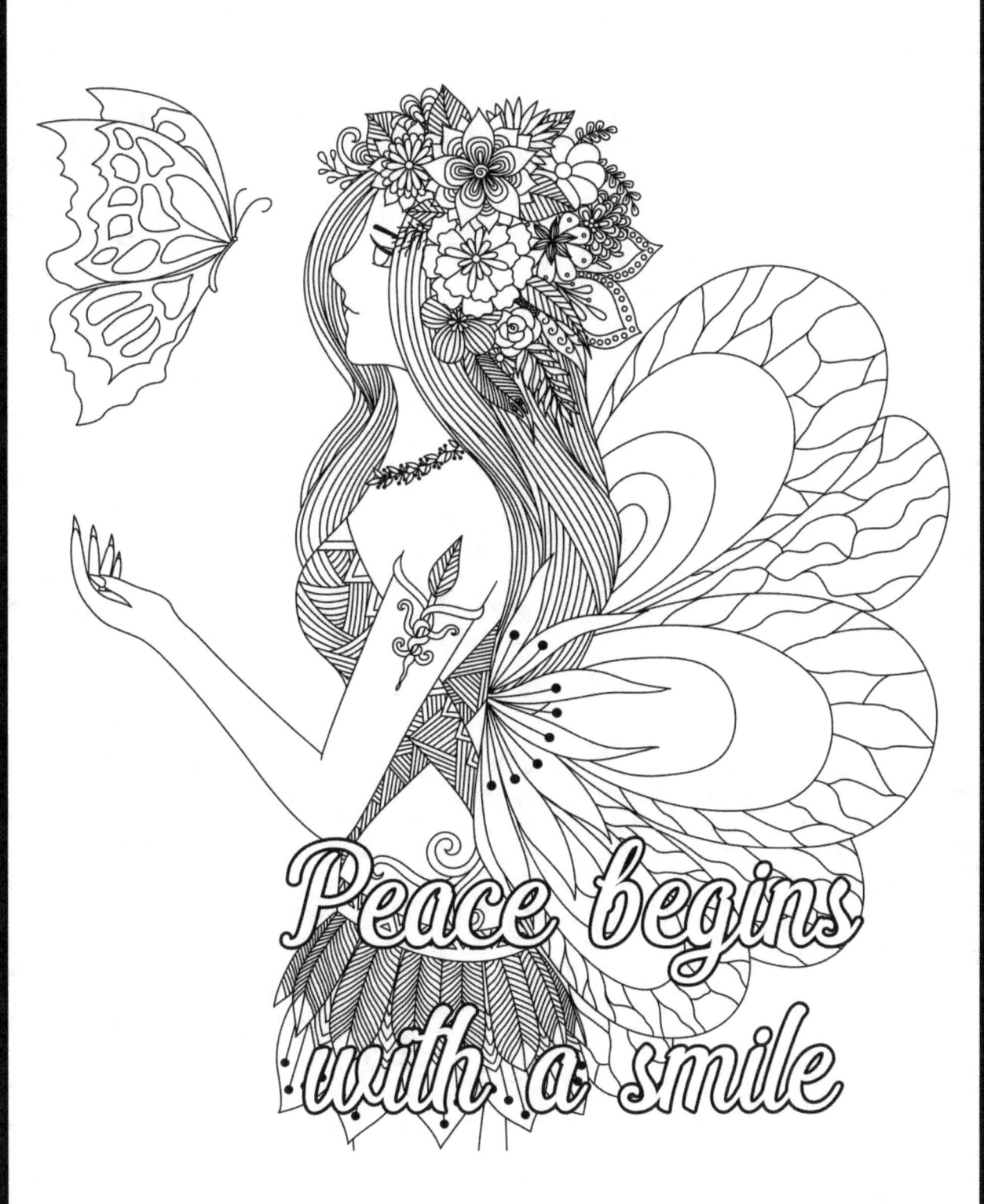

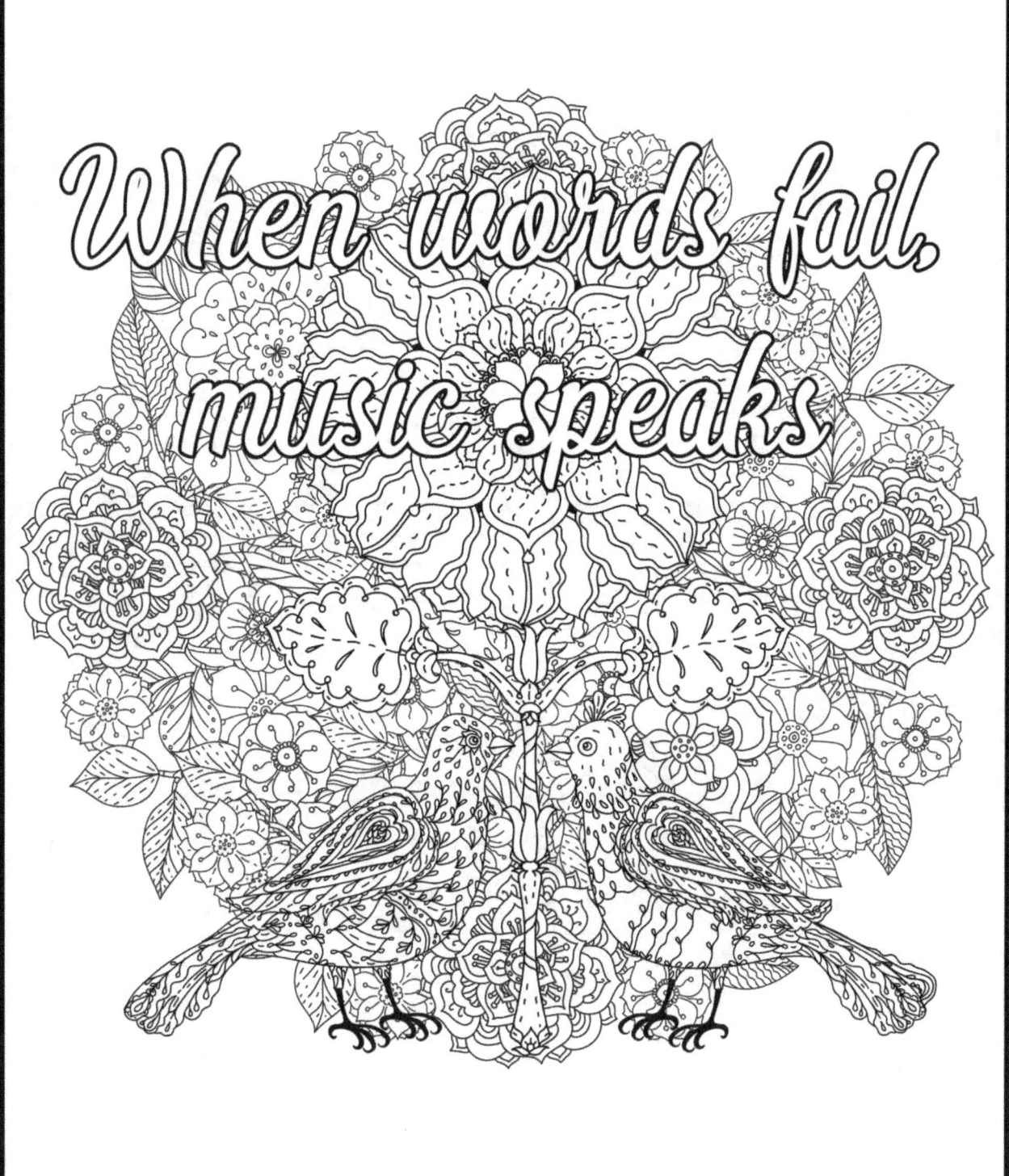

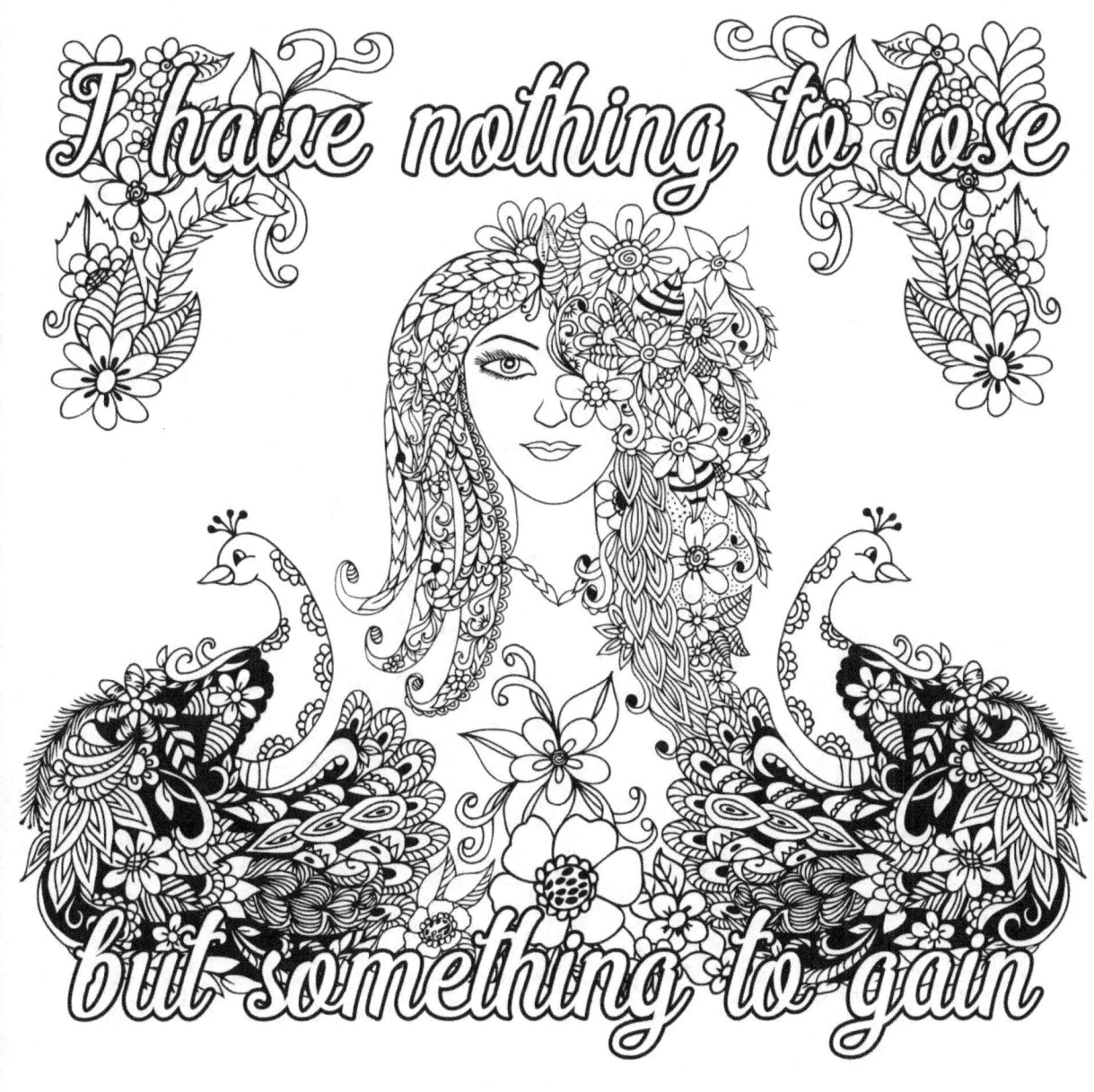

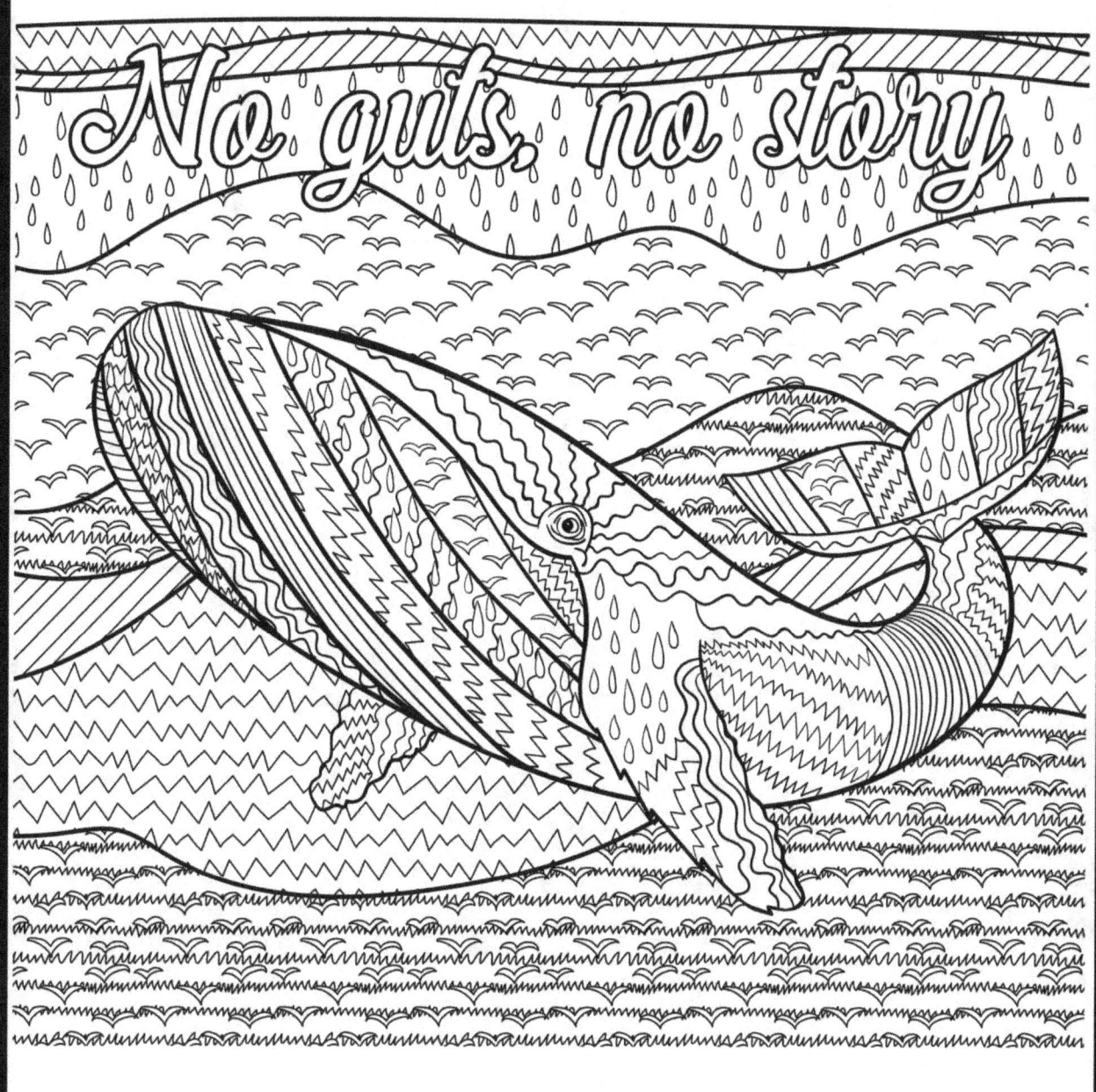

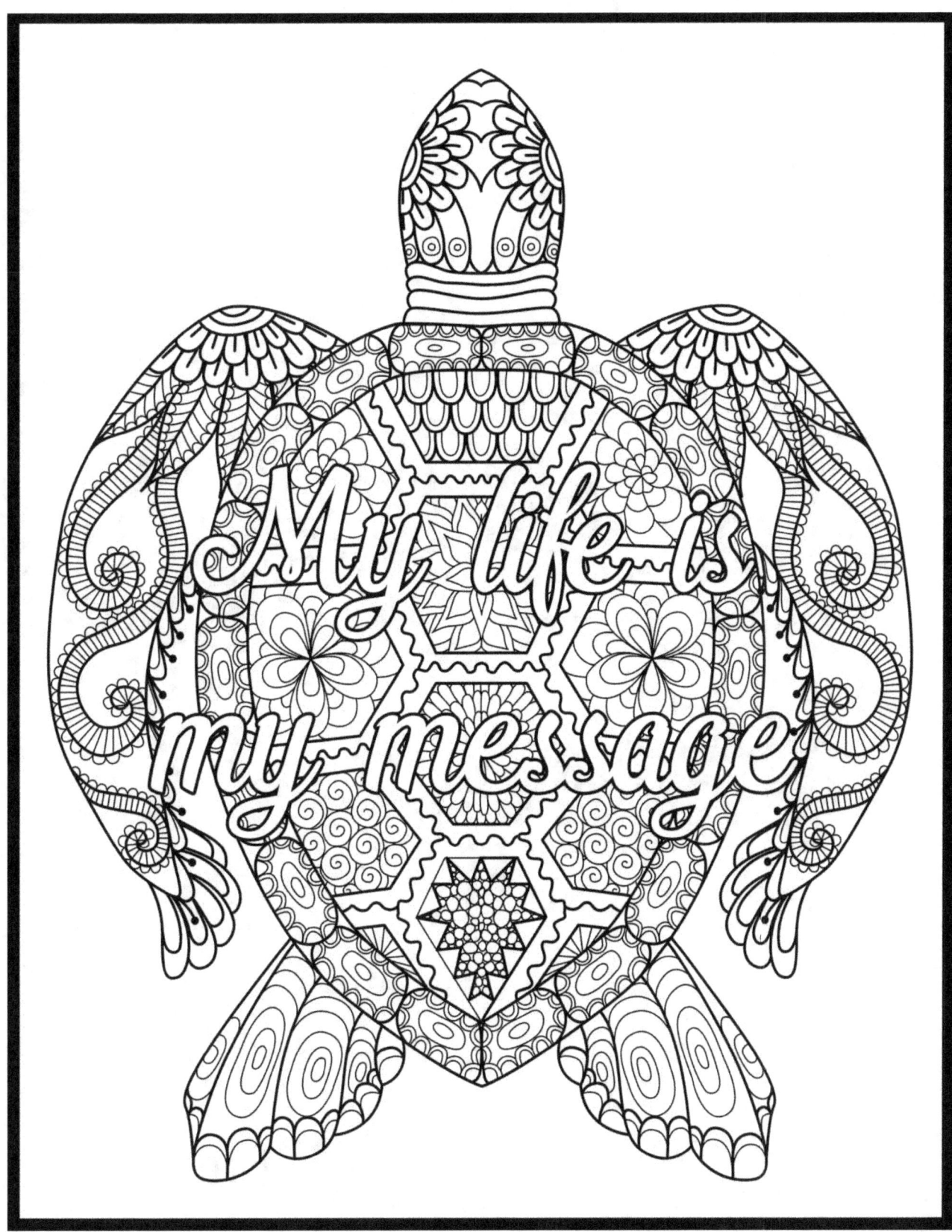

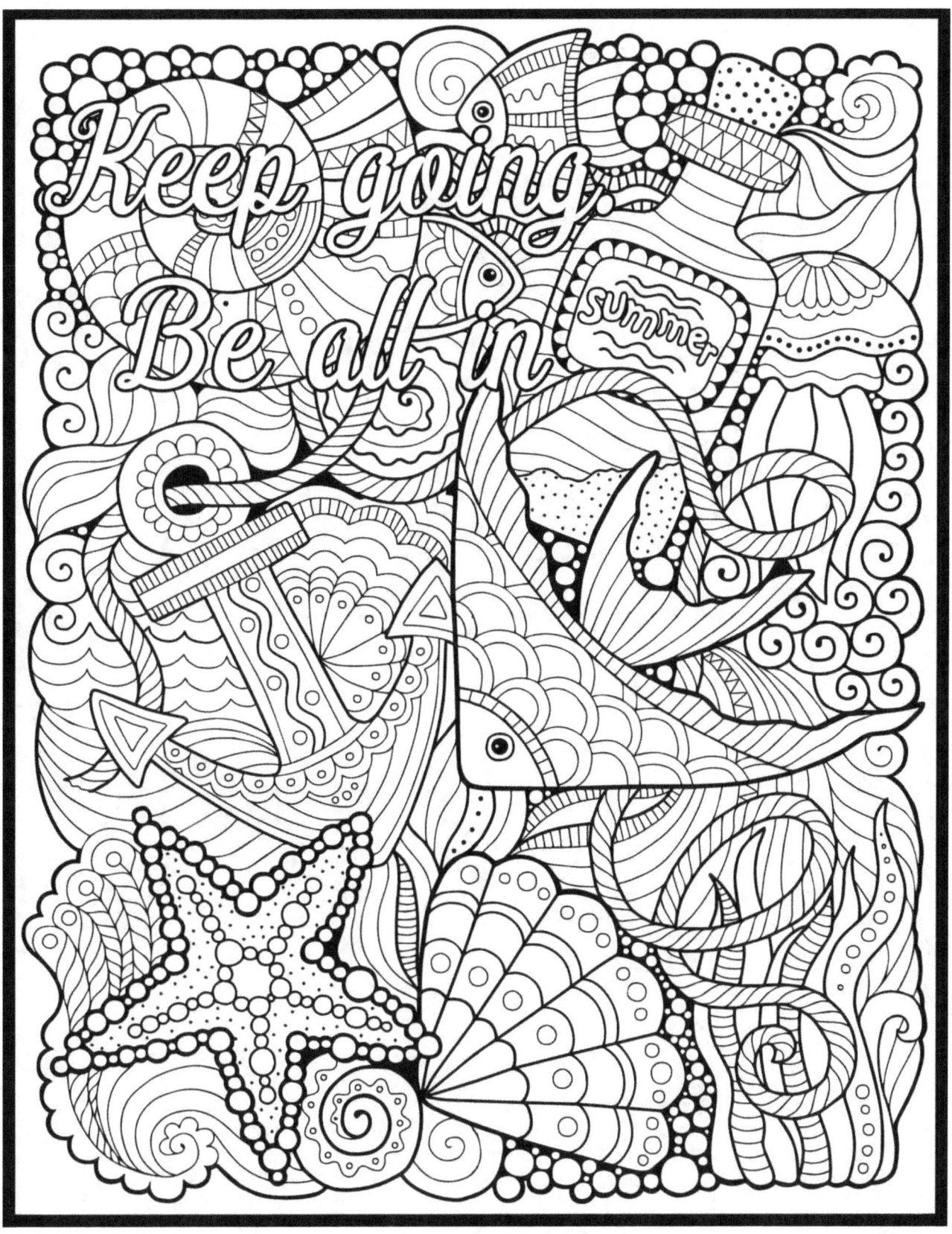

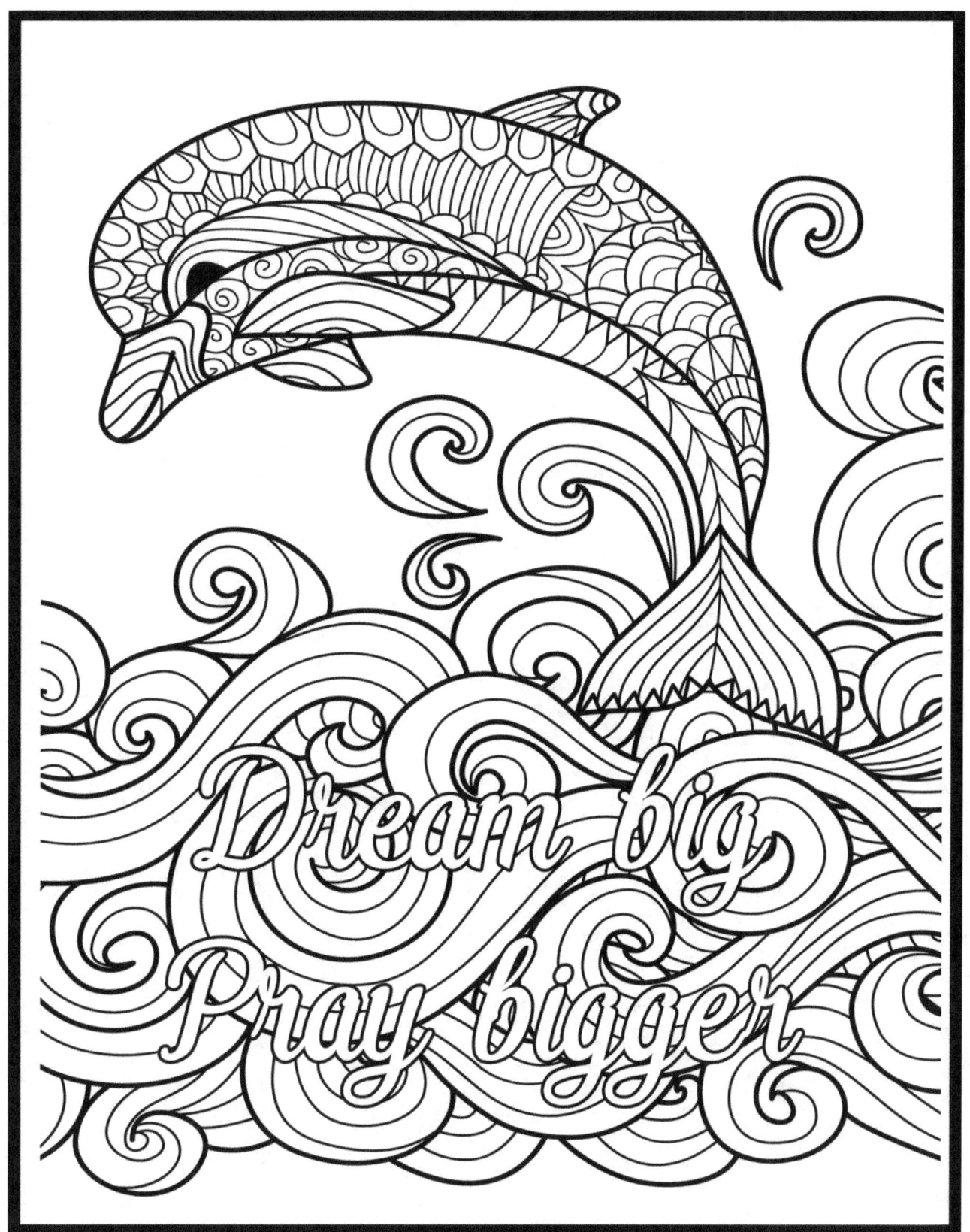

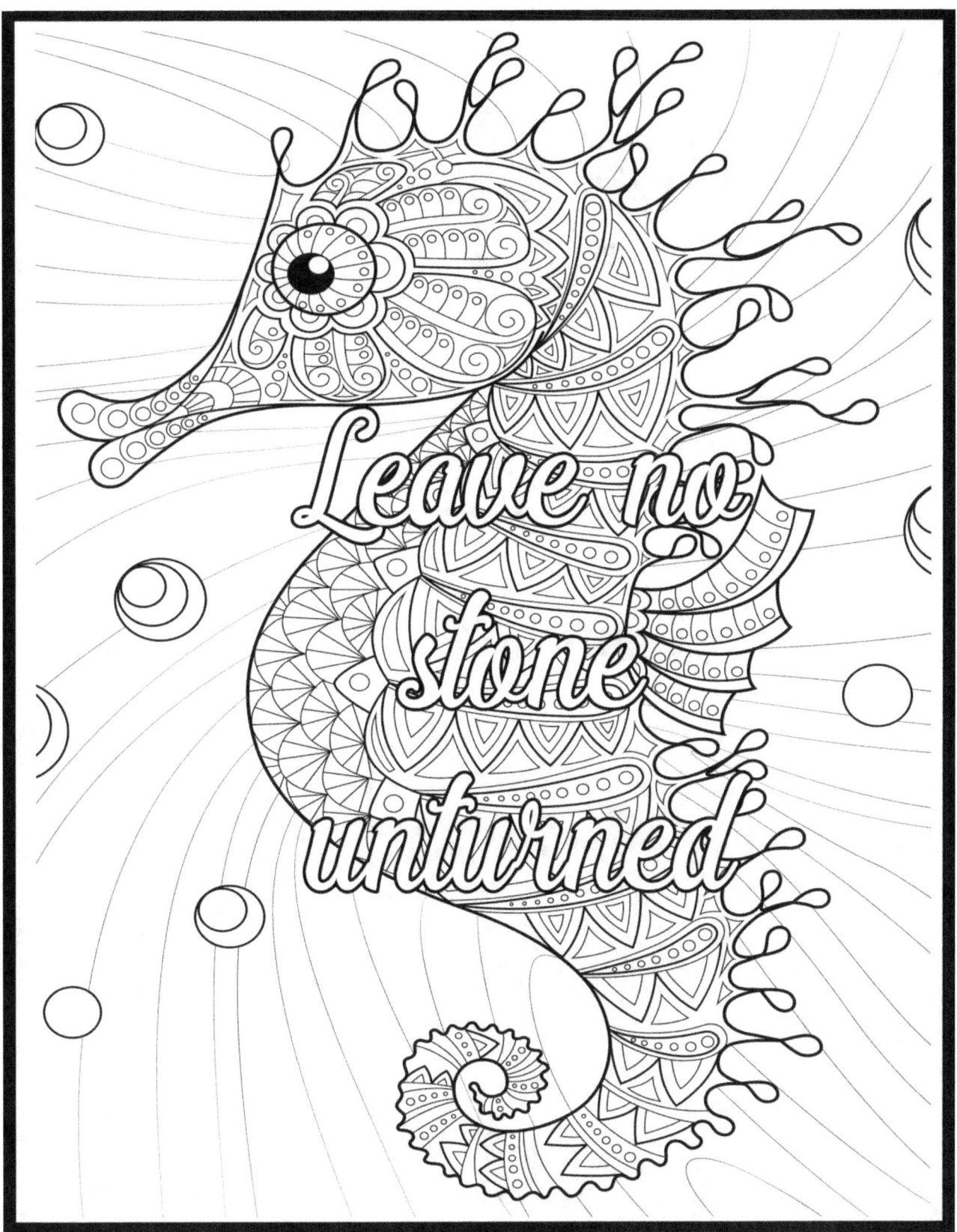

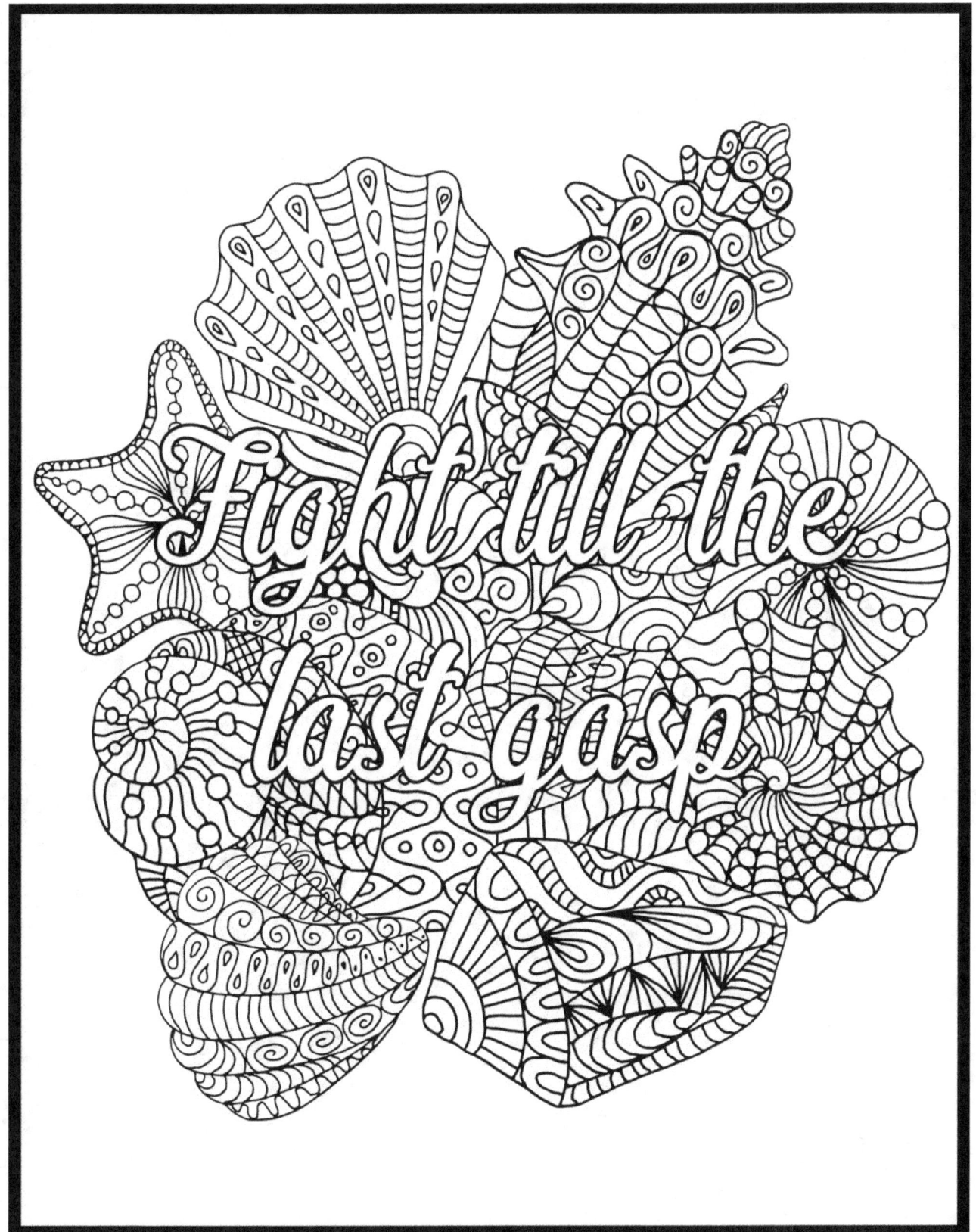

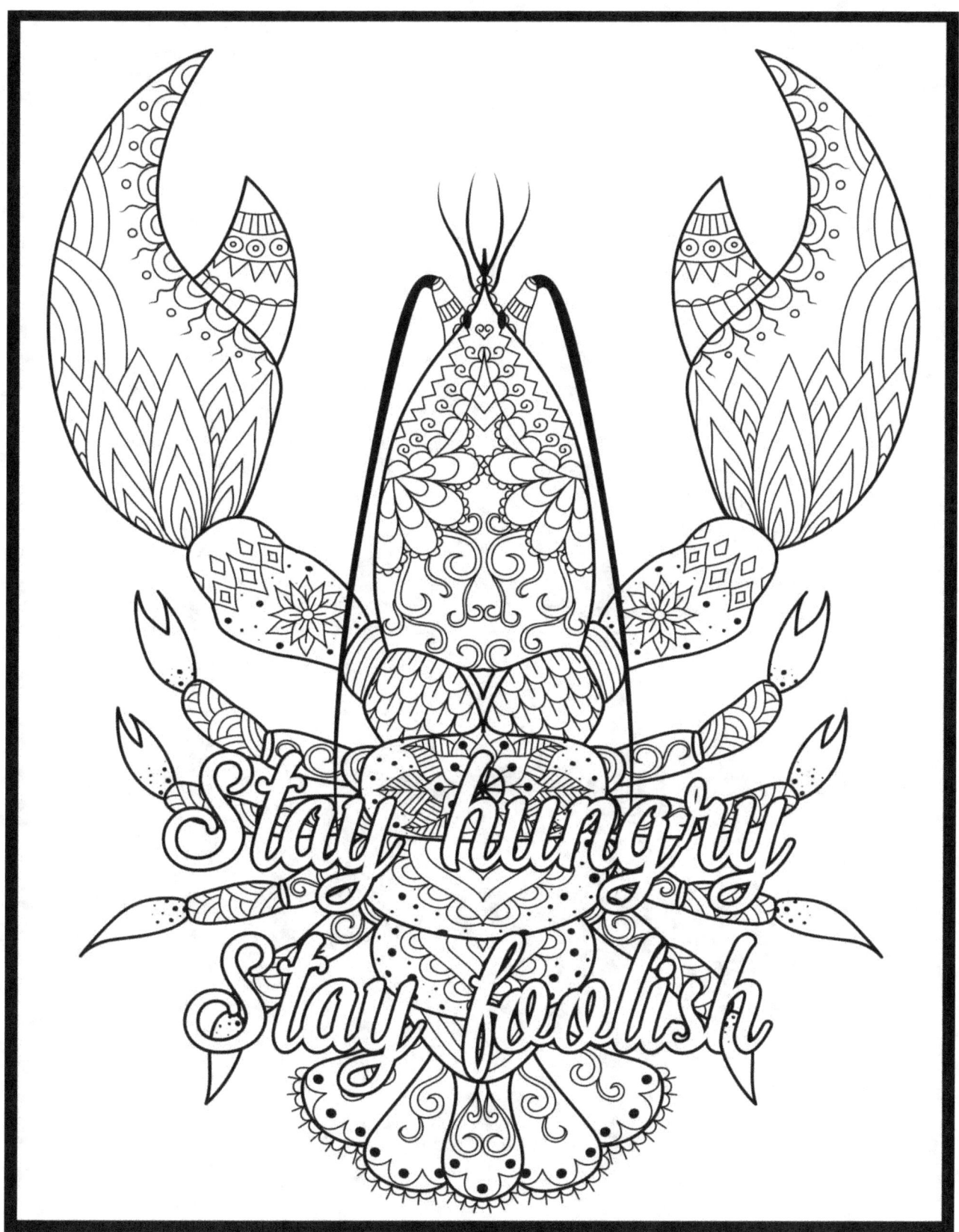

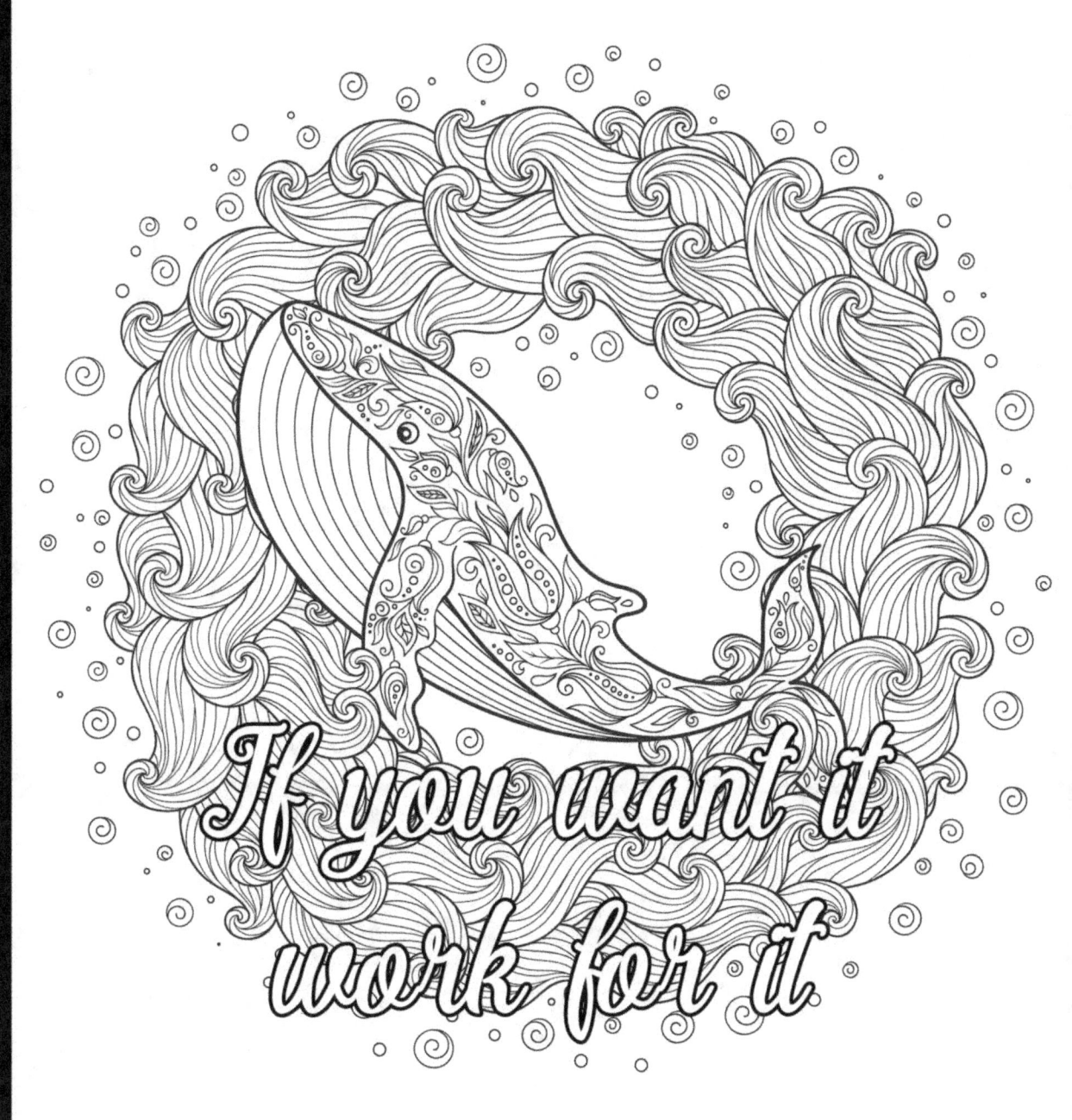

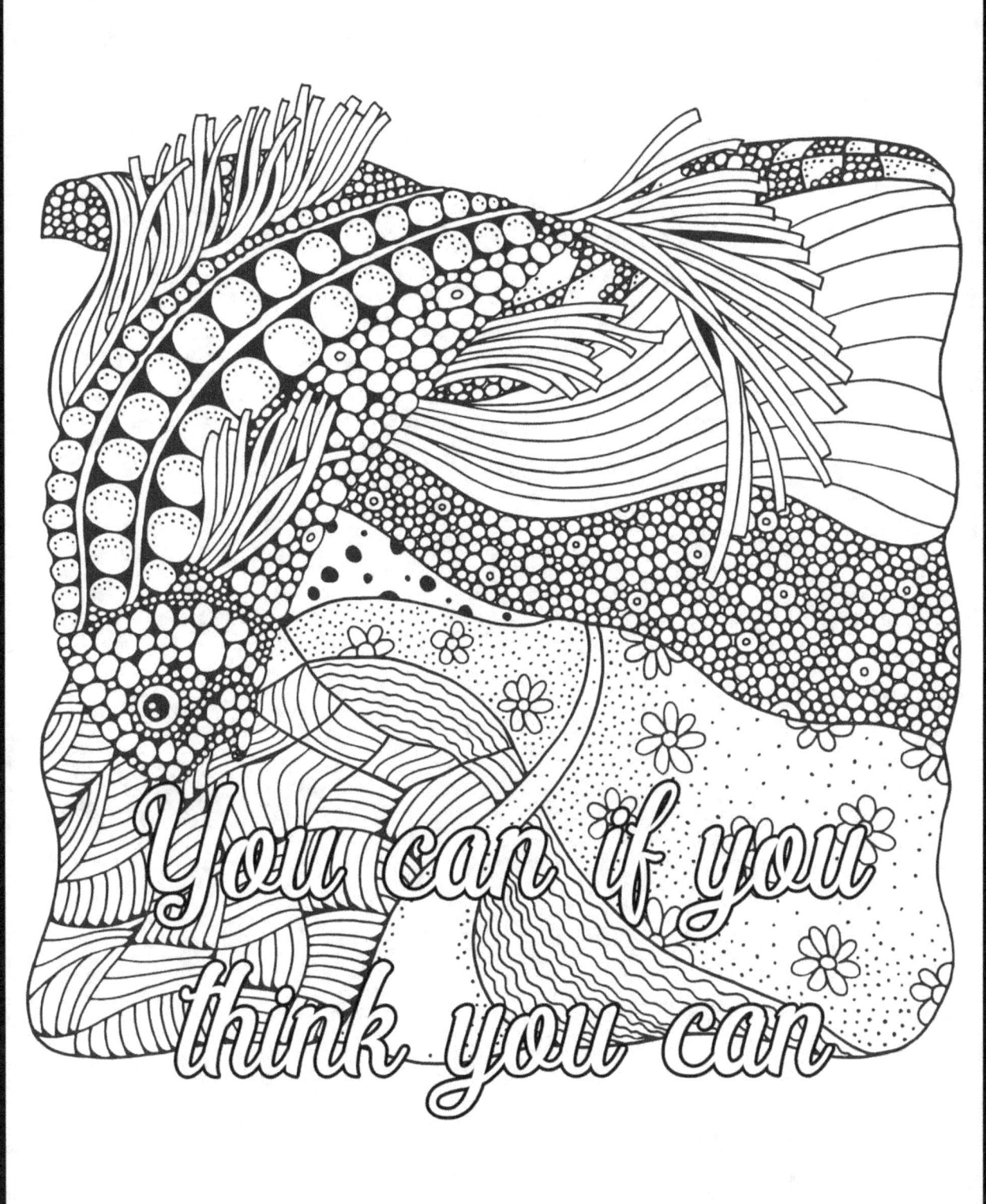

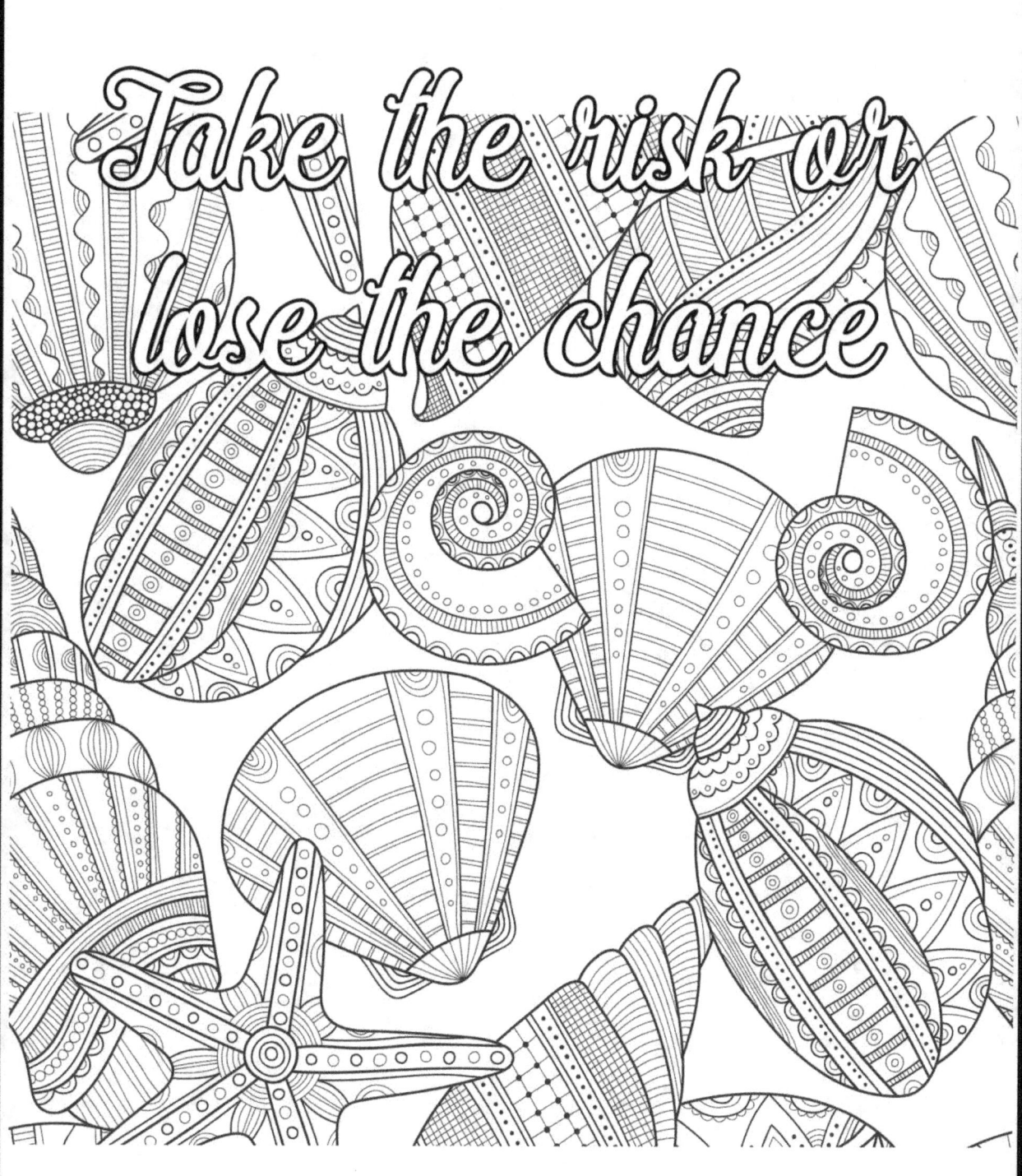

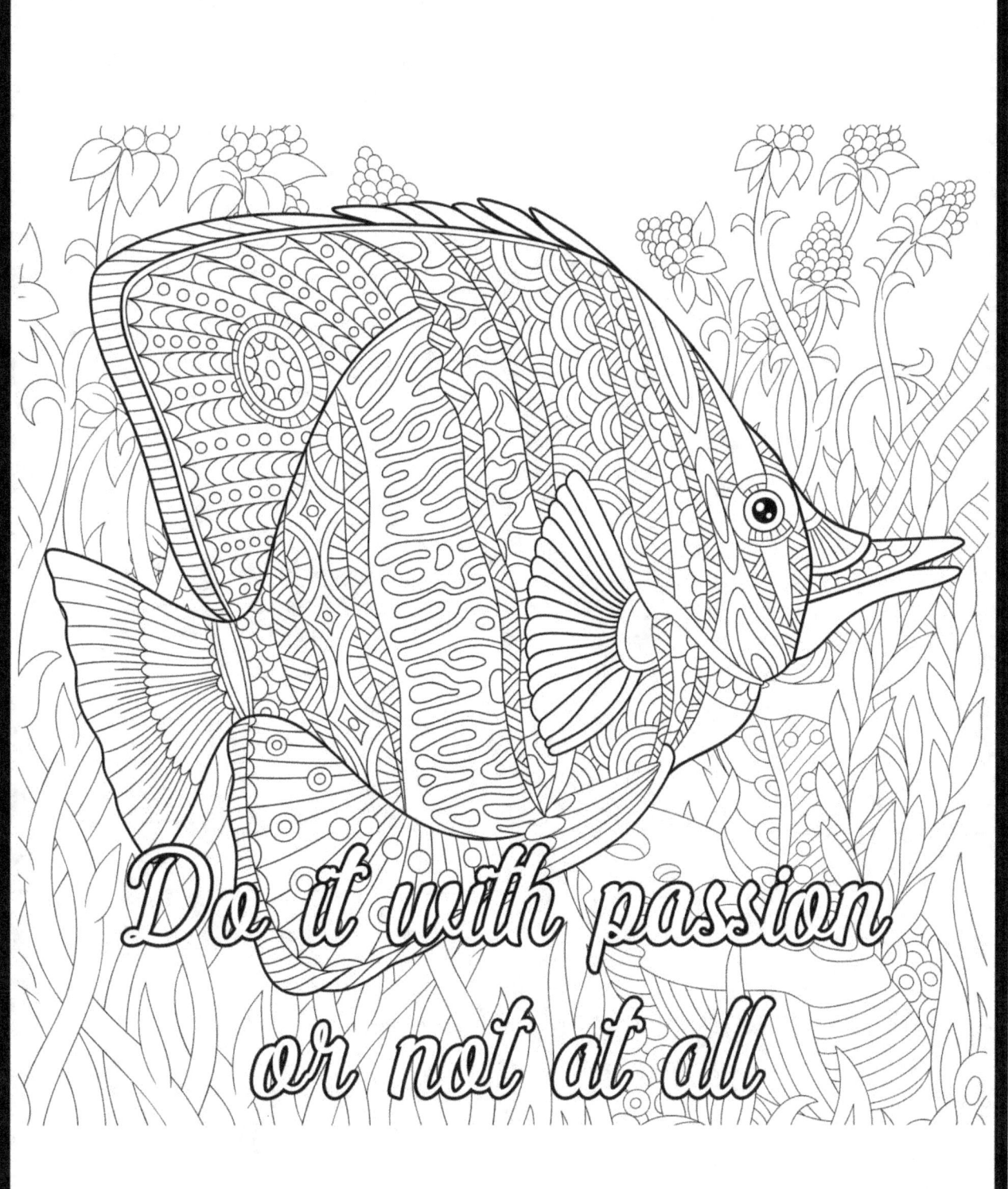

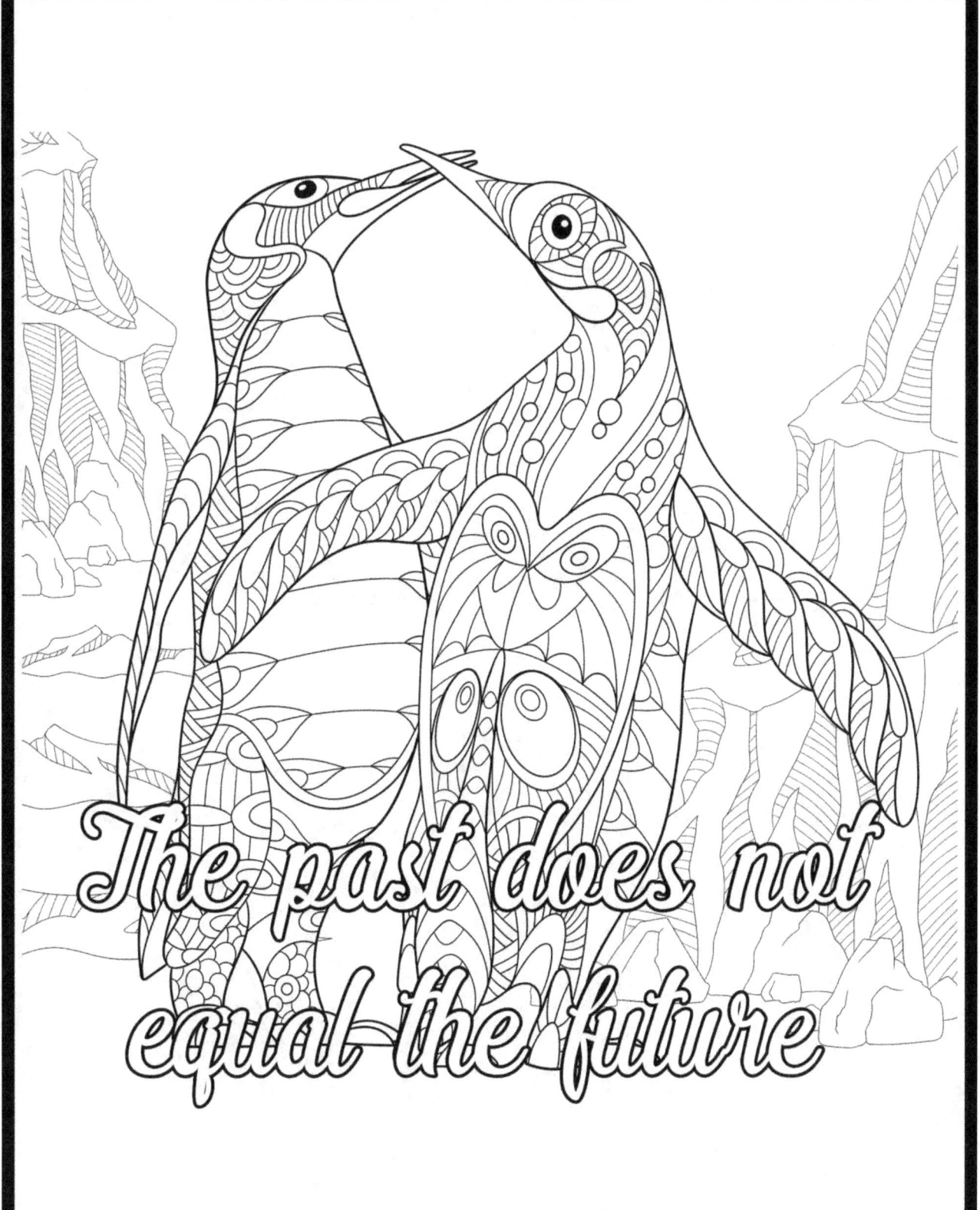

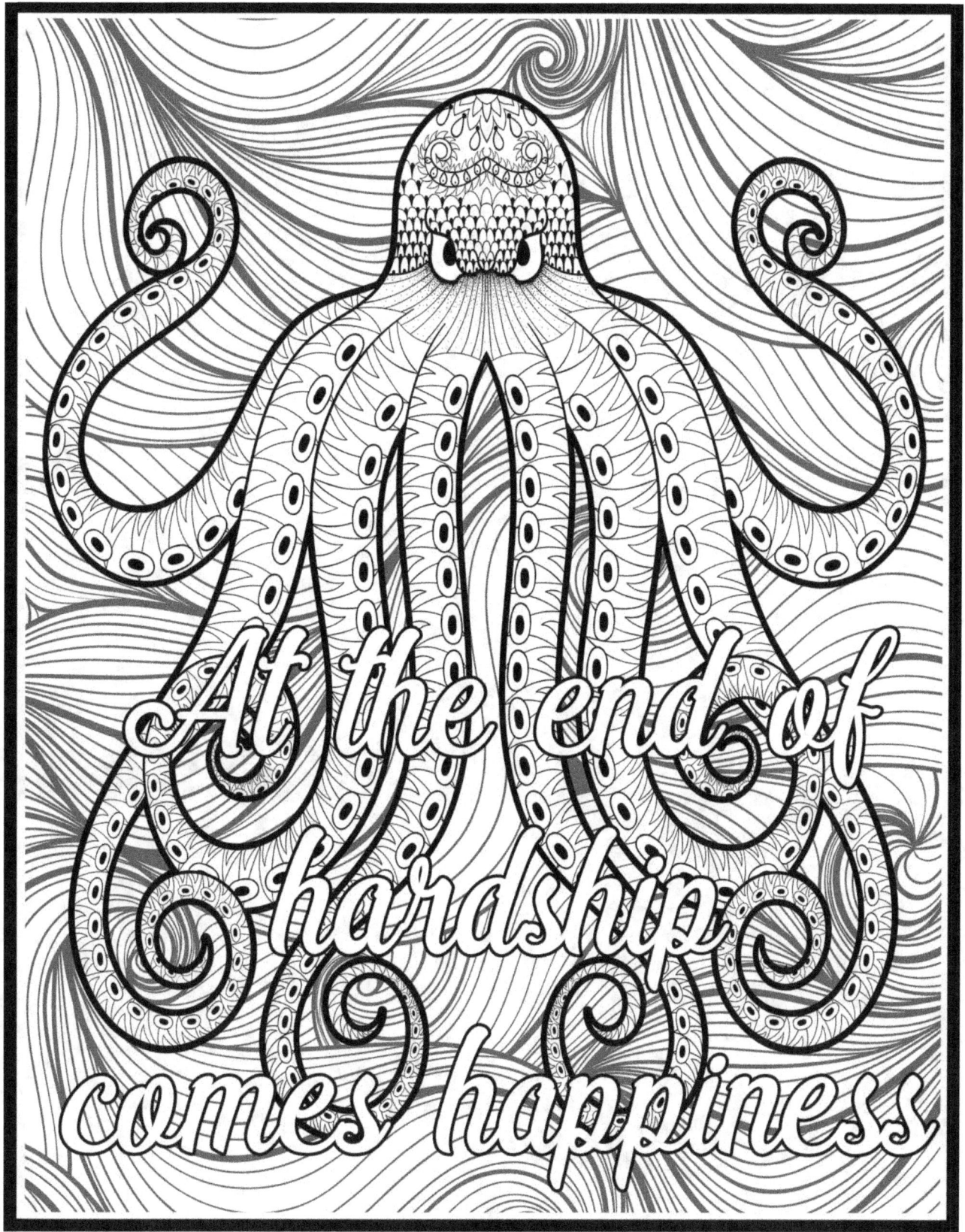

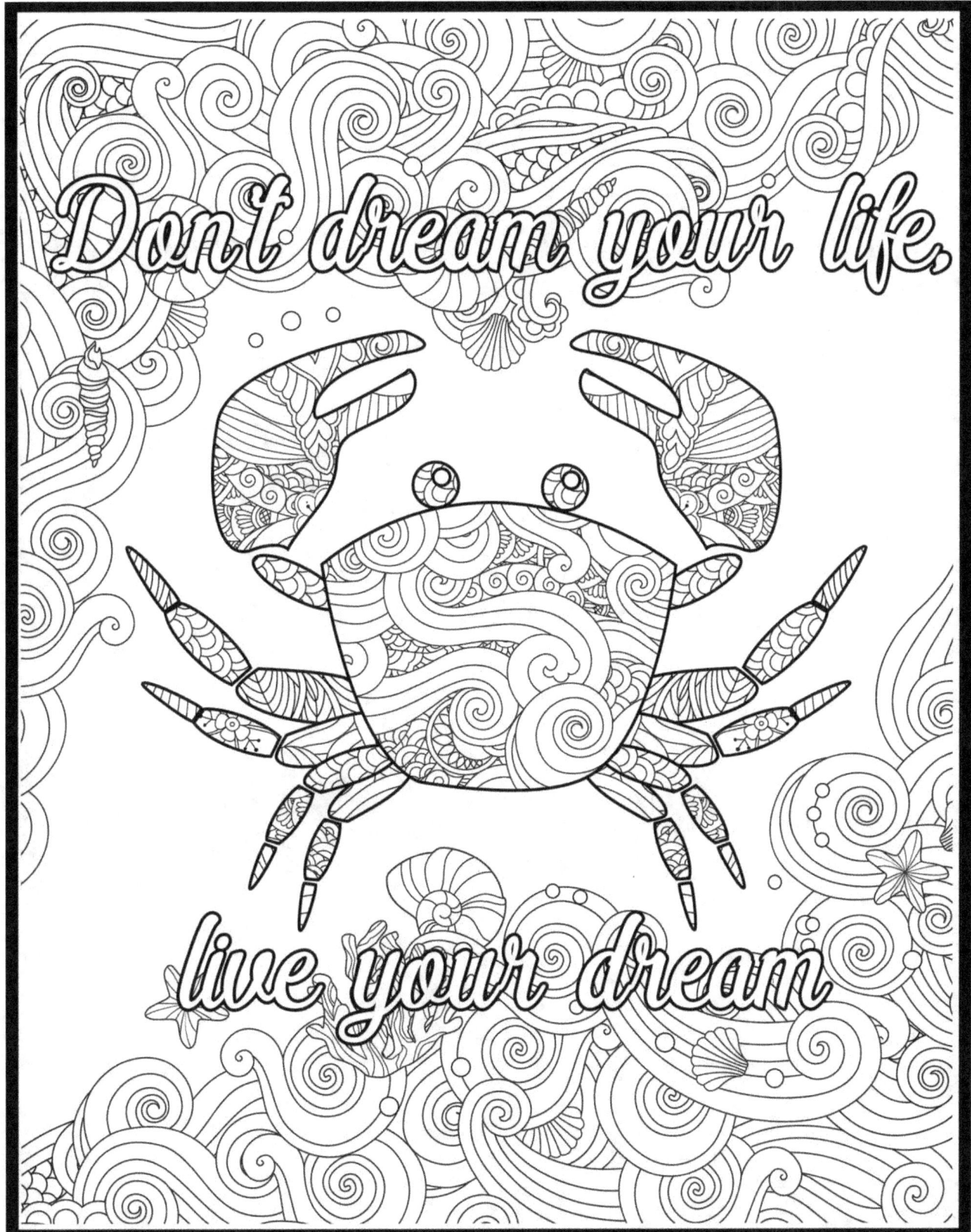

Dream without fear

Love without limits

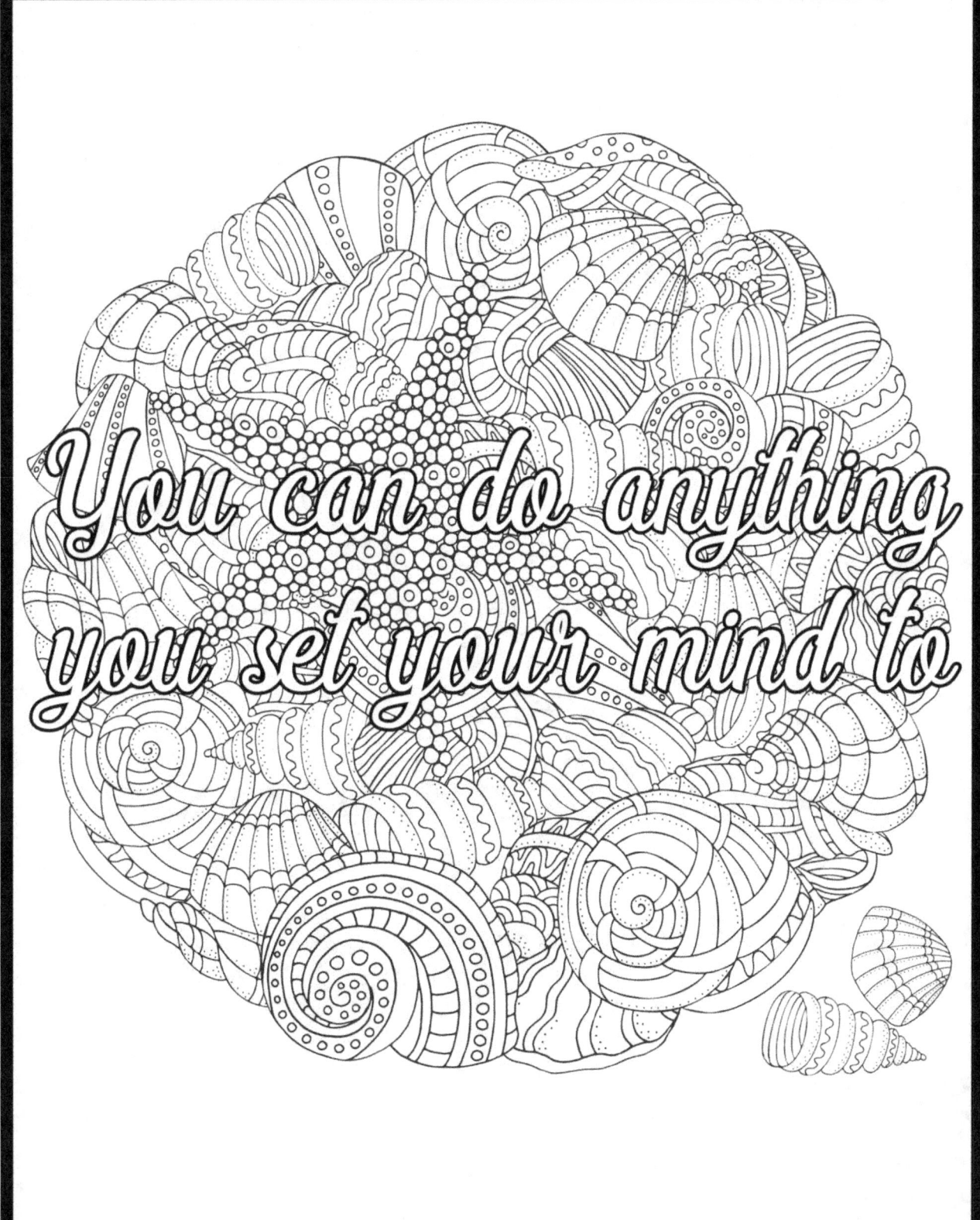

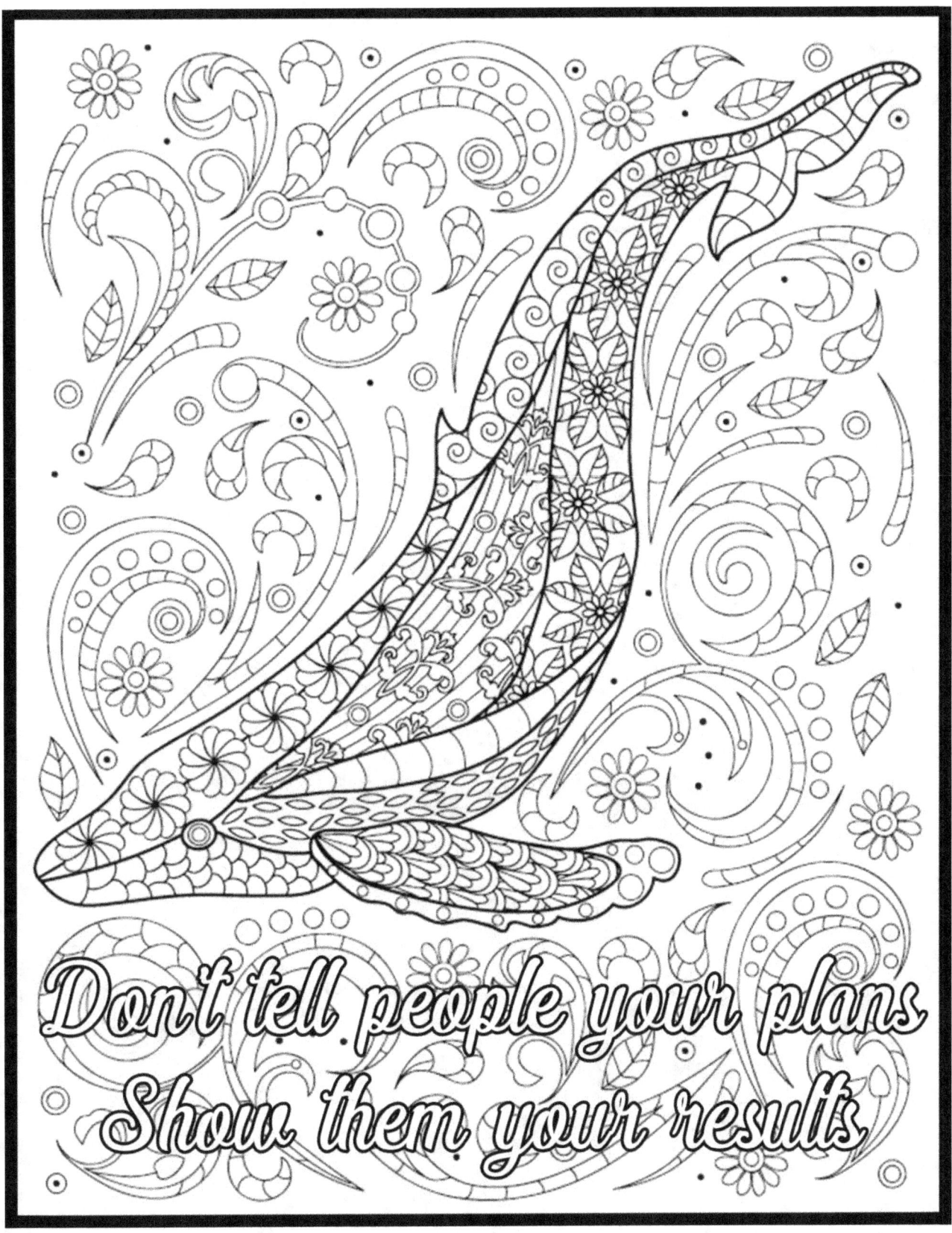

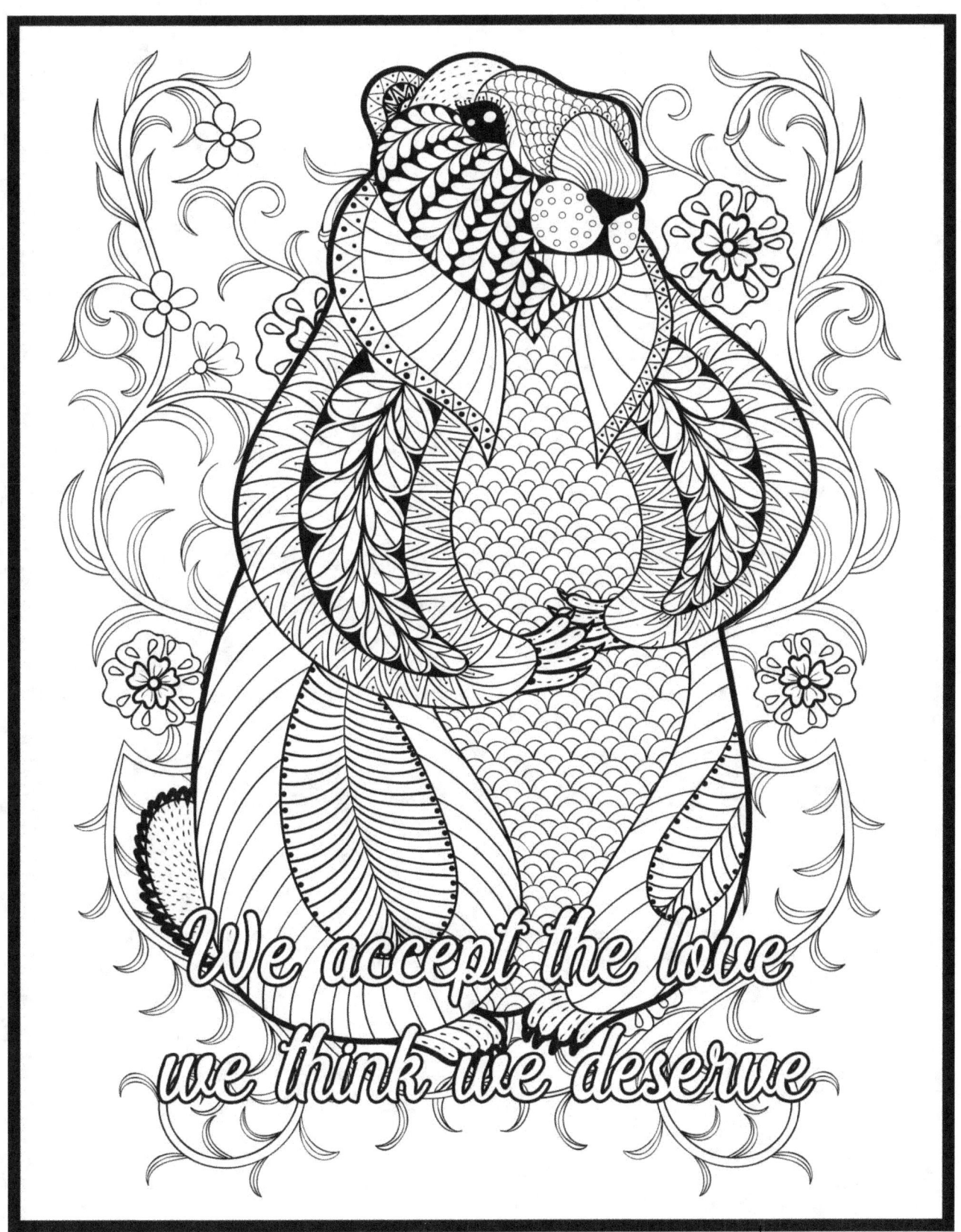

We accept the love
we think we deserve

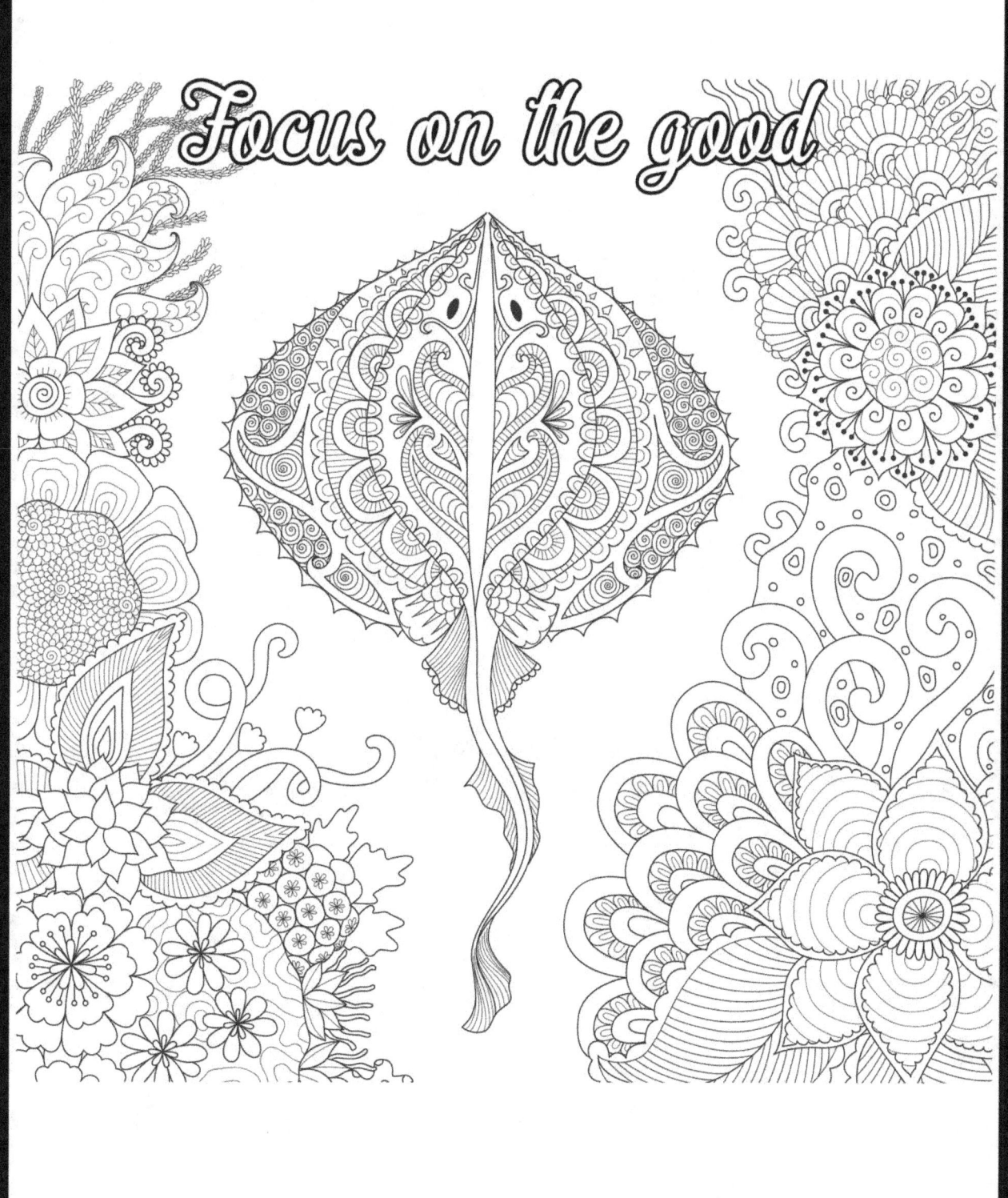

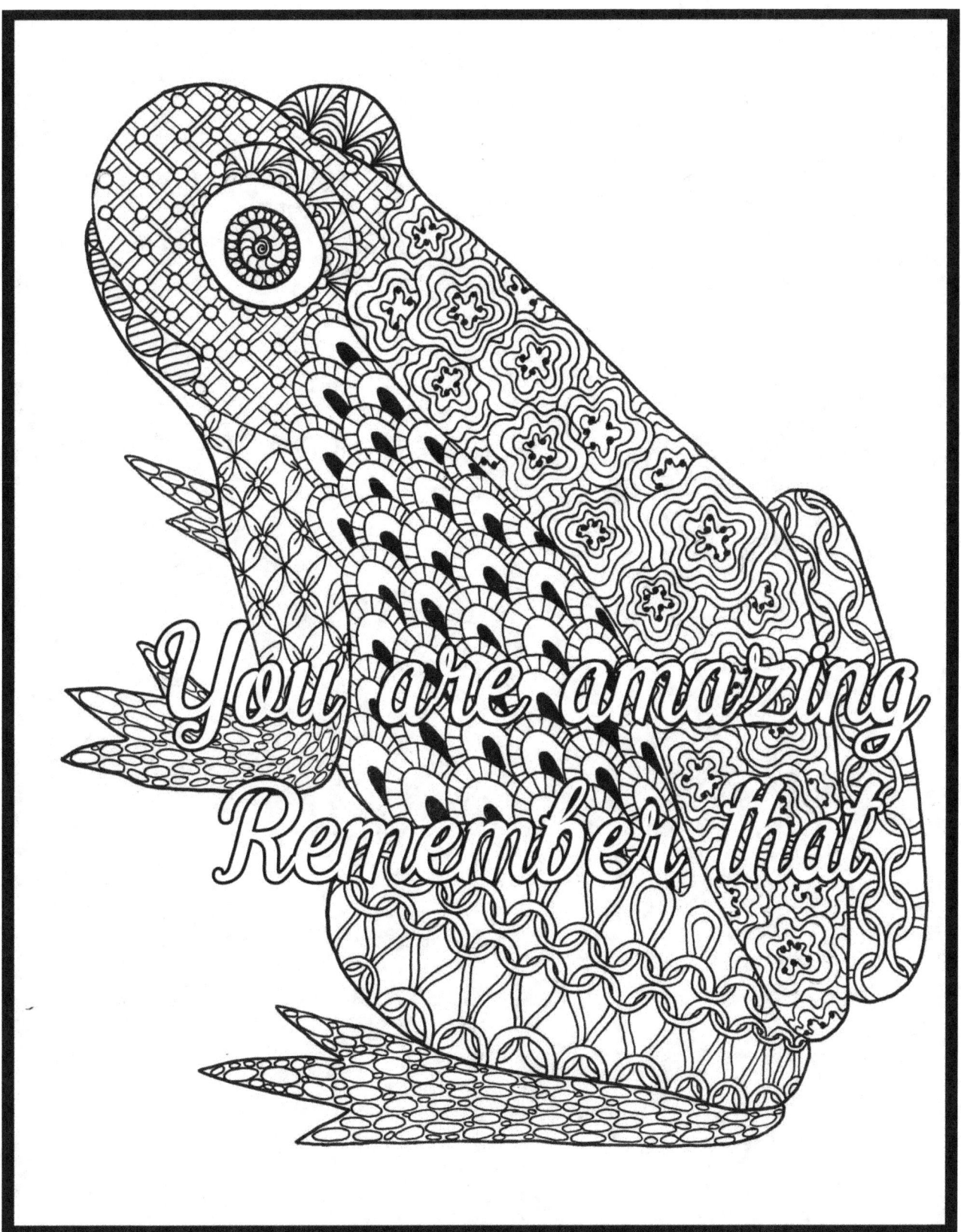

www.ingramcontent.com/pod-product-compliance
Lightning Source LLC
Chambersburg PA
CBHW081608220526
45468CB00010B/2809